Sarah Peer

KATHARINE BLAKE

THE UNINNOCENT

Katharine Blake is an adjunct professor at Vermont Law School's Center for Justice Reform. She received her JD, with pro bono distinction, from Stanford Law School, where she was an editor of the *Stanford Law & Policy Review*. She has taught English in San Quentin State Prison and served as the director of special projects for the Children's Defense Fund. She lives with her family in Virginia.

THE

UNINNOCENT

THE

UNINNOCENT

NOTES ON

VIOLENCE AND

MERCY

KATHARINE BLAKE

FSG ORIGINALS
FARRAR, STRAUS AND GIROUX
NEW YORK

FSG Originals
Farrar, Straus and Giroux
120 Broadway, New York 10271

Owing to limitations of space, all acknowledgments for permission to reprint previously published material can be found on page 210.

Library of Congress Cataloging-in-Publication Data
Names: Blake, Katharine, 1984– author.
Title: The uninnocent : notes on violence and mercy / Katharine Blake.
Description: First edition. | New York : FSG Originals / Farrar, Straus and
    Giroux, 2021. | Includes bibliographical references.
Identifiers: LCCN 2021025275 | ISBN 9780374538521 (paperback)
Subjects: LCSH: Blake, Katharine, 1984– | Prisoners' families—United
    States—Biography. | Lawyers—United States—Biography. | Justice. |
    Criminal justice, Administration of—United States.
Classification: LCC HV8885 .B53 2021 | DDC 306.85086/927—dc23
LC record available at https://lccn.loc.gov/2021025275

Designed by Janet Evans-Scanlon

Our books may be purchased in bulk for promotional, educational,
or business use. Please contact your local bookseller or the Macmillan
Corporate and Premium Sales Department at 1-800-221-7945, extension
5442, or by email at MacmillanSpecialMarkets@macmillan.com.

www.fsgoriginals.com • www.fsgbooks.com
Follow us on Twitter, Facebook, and Instagram at @fsgoriginals

10 9 8 7 6 5 4 3 2 1

In memory of Michael Downing,
1958–2021

It began to seem that one would have to hold in the mind forever two ideas which seemed to be in opposition. The first idea was acceptance, the acceptance, totally without rancor, of life as it is, and men as they are: in the light of this idea, it goes without saying that injustice is a commonplace. But . . . the second idea was of equal power: that one must never, in one's own life, accept these injustices as commonplace but must fight them with all one's strength. This fight begins, however, in the heart.

—JAMES BALDWIN, *Notes of a Native Son*

I have set before you life and death, blessing and curse; therefore choose life.

—DEUTERONOMY 30:19

AUTHOR'S NOTE

This is a work of creative nonfiction. Events and conversations capture the substance of experience, but are not held out as literal representations. As for the crime involving members of my family, all of the names and many identifying details have been changed in the interest of privacy. I've drawn facts from publicly available information and my own research. The views expressed are mine, and so are the experiences, except to the extent I write about the heartbreak of others, in which case I am a visitor and witness, not a protagonist.

CONTENTS

PART I

HOW DO WE
GO ON

---

no one
no window

black water
nail-scratched walls

your pure face turned away
embarrassed

you
who the earth was for.

—JEAN VALENTINE,
"In prison"

What Didion wrote about San Francisco but also America more broadly was still true: the center was not holding. In her day, it was Vietnam and LSD, racism and assassination. Four decades later it was tent cities and evictions, opioids and meth, school shootings and racism and prisons filled to their literal ceilings with bodies.

I was born in San Francisco, and in my late twenties I moved back after spending most of my life on the East Coast. The move was for a man I loved, still love, but I didn't love San Francisco. The topography made me tense, as if I might topple backward at the crest of each steep hill. As if the houses nestled into hillsides might start sliding.

The year before, I'd graduated from law school and then worked for the Children's Defense Fund in D.C., and when I left that job for San Francisco, it was for love, but also because I'd lost hope. The shooting at Sandy Hook Elementary School, during which Adam Lanza had killed twenty-six people, mostly children, had thrown us into a fight for federal gun safety measures, and when we lost that fight, I was angry and disheartened. Around the same time, my sixteen-year-old cousin, Scott, who'd had a mental break and murdered a child, was being tried as an adult and facing life in prison without parole. The world of the law that I'd studied and worked to be a part of seemed irredeemable.

I'm not proud of losing hope—it smacks of weakness. Others have kept theirs in scenarios a thousand times more harrowing and grave. I didn't yet know that hope is nothing less than a discipline. In any case, bitterness opened the door for me to leave.

But also I left for love. I wanted to make a home and a family. I wanted to see if I could make a family different from the one I'd been raised in, which was not an original desire. My mother and father had tried to do this, and maybe their parents had, too, in their own confounded ways. Now it was my turn. And leaving D.C. for the man I loved (I'll call him L) seemed like an elemental step in this enduring desire.

After a long search, L finally found a tiny, whitewashed one-bedroom for us in the Castro, a neighborhood that was not socked in by fog the way others were. Our lives were sunsoaked. But in other ways—down certain streets and alleys and around some corners—San Francisco swirled with apocalyptic darkness.

Through the wide bay windows in the bedroom of that apartment, we watched the light change over the face of Corona Heights and listened to the sounds of people living on the street below. We listened to their yelling, swearing, laughing, and fighting each night as we went to sleep. Marijuana smoke drifted through our windows. The perimeter of our building always smelled like piss.

In the early morning, as I stepped over sleeping bodies stretched out on flattened cardboard boxes, arms and legs like commas punctuating the sidewalks, I thought of the parents I'd met while fighting for gun legislation, the living cautionary tales meant to put a human face on gun death. All those parents who were missing their children, and here, the second line of the couplet—all these children on the streets of San Francisco, missing from somewhere else.

There was a stretch of days when a young man sobbed inconsolably as he paced up and down the block each afternoon. Once or twice, he threw his slender body on the sidewalk and beat his fists against the pavement.

What troubled me was the chaos—not just the chaos of unhomed lives but the chaos of fate that they suggested. I couldn't shake the feeling that it all boiled down to chance. That I was the one who ended up sleeping on clean white sheets and not on cardboard boxes felt like nothing more than luck. I couldn't find any sense of order, divine or otherwise.

Shortly after moving to San Francisco, I started teaching at San Quentin State Prison. The course curriculum covered everything from grammar to composition to how to write a five-paragraph essay and cite sources. In practicing these skills, the men wrote often about their lives before prison, about the women who raised them, their mothers and grandmothers. One wrote about how it felt to get the call that his mother had died while he was locked up and he couldn't say goodbye. Another wrote about the crime that put him in prison—he'd shot the guy who'd killed his little brother—and the way he felt he'd let his mother down because now she was alone. The catch-22: he would have let her down if he hadn't avenged the death. The cellblocks in the prison were like library stacks, rows and rows of stories down every dimly lit hall.

San Quentin Prison is settled on the shore of the San Francisco Bay between Mill Valley and San Rafael, some of the most scenic real estate in the country. A three-bedroom home ten minutes from the prison will sell for no less—and usually much more—than a million dollars. As I walked from the parking lot to the first clearance gate, the disequilibrium of the barbed wire and armed watchtower against the bay at dusk always made me hold my breath.

Just as I held my breath in the city, so full of suffering as it was. Which is to say, there was a link between the city and the prison. Between the bodies I stepped over in the street as I walked to my car to drive to San Quentin and the caged bodies in the yard once I arrived. Homelessness and incarceration represent two points on a circle, both characterized by a lack of privacy and, paradoxically, invisibility. They also share the condition of something broken. Lives bent and bowed, histories of heartbreak.

It was in those days of traveling between San Francisco

and San Quentin that I started keeping track of heartbreak. I know I was thinking of Scott when I did.

My cousin Scott was a rising junior in high school when he killed a nine-year-old boy he'd never met named Ryan. The night I started thinking about heartbreak, I was thinking of Scott because I heard on the car radio that Creigh Deeds, a Virginia state senator, had been attacked by his son, Gus, who had been diagnosed with bipolar disorder. Gus had stabbed his father in the face and chest and then shot himself. I'd met Senator Deeds years earlier when I was working on a political campaign in Virginia. I remembered his kind blue eyes. I tried to imagine those eyes with a scar running between them.

When I heard about Creigh Deeds, I was driving through Haight-Ashbury on my way back from San Quentin. In light of the attack, *your host Rachel Martin* was interviewing another father of a son with mental illness. *There is a debate in this country about mental health and resources*, she said. *Are people getting the access to care that they need?* The father said simply, no, people were not getting the care they needed. And then he said: *I don't know the whole story and probably never will, but the tragedies never end.*

The tragedies never end.

Of course when the man said those words, he was talking about Creigh Deeds, but to me it sounded like more. A thesis, a catchall. It was both personal (a phrase pulled from the depths of his own pain with his own son) and general (a comment on the endlessness of suffering). It was shorthand for how the world looked after Scott's crime, a feeling that filled my days and nights in San Francisco. It was how I felt when I stepped over sleeping bodies and heard fighting below our windows and walked past the old gas chamber at San Quentin. It's how I felt when I got a letter from Scott with the return address marked *Death Row*. The tragedies never end. So how do we go on?

That night, when I got home, I opened a Word document and typed it out: *the tragedies never end*.

At the top of the page I wrote *HEARTBREAK*. And then I stared at it. The word surprised me. It wasn't one I'd thought about very much before, but in that moment, I was struck by its precision. It felt good to have a word. I don't mean that I thought my heart was broken—though I think now that it was; I think having your heart broken is as easy as listening to the news or trying to love the world— rather, I mean it's what I'd been seeing when I looked out my window. My literal window, but also that broader, metaphorical one that defines any worldview. *Heartbreak* was a word for the pain I saw in families and systems, homelessness and violence, courtrooms and prisons. It was the cause and effect of that pain. And though I would not have said then that my heart was broken, I knew enough to know that the pain I carried inside my own body collected in my chest.

The document grew and grew. Over weeks and months and years, I copied sentences from books and poems and plays, conversations with friends, headlines, and studies about hearts—anything that shed light on the nebulous and to my mind misunderstood concept of heartbreak. I wrote down questions. Where did the word come from, why does it mean so many things, how do you keep your heart intact, how do you go on after it breaks, what does justice look like for the brokenhearted, what does it mean to heal, do you inherit the heartbreak of generations past?

What you look for you will see. Big red slashes of heartbreak out in the world. A shooting. A fire. A failed reconciliation. War and hunger. And then it started echoing down the corridors of my own family history, which brought the past disconcertingly into the present. At night my mind followed the threads between memories and images, unperturbed by time or logic:

Mothers and fathers wait in a room at the
Newtown fire station to find out if their children
made it out alive

A blond boy, who looks like my brother, sleeps in
the shadows behind my building

My mother's brother Roy lies shot and bleeding under
a streetlight on a hot Texas night

Michael Brown's body lies shot and bleeding on a street
for hours

Scott is covered in Ryan's blood

In his obituary photo, Ryan is dressed in a white button-down shirt, smiling

My brother's smile fades when the other boys move away from him at lunchtime because he was born missing a hand, a bird's broken wing

My father is drinking a scotch

My father is angry, chasing me up the stairs

My father is taking a swing at his father with a two-by-four, and the dust rises in the scuffle

I am drunk, crying on a bathroom floor

My great-grandmother is crying on a bathroom floor, holding the body of her husband, my great-grandfather, who'd put a bullet through his head

Scott's mug shot flashes across the evening news while oil spills into the ocean like ink—

I am trying to describe a feeling. When time collapses and the edges of experience and history bleed together into something that casts a shadow. For me this shadow took the shape of heartbreak. And I started writing about it because I thought writing might help me understand it, and I thought that understanding might protect me. Proust writes: *Ideas come to us as the successors to griefs, and griefs, at the moment when they change into ideas, lose some part of their power to injure our heart.* This was my half-formed hope.

EARLY DEPICTIONS OF THE BROKEN HEART, I FOUND, were literal. Cave paintings, dating back to the Ice Age, in which a heart-shaped object is skewered by a spear. The first known instances of the idea as metaphor appear in Sumerian proverbs carved into stone tablets some five thousand years ago:

> *My fingernail that hurts is clutched in my embrace.*
> *My foot that hurts is in my sandal. But who will*
> *find my aching heart?*
>
> *May Inanna pour oil on my heart that aches.*

Then came Eros, or Cupid, who shot arrows through his victims' hearts. His golden-tipped arrows made you fall in love, but his lead-tipped arrows inspired disgust. In both cases, the outcome was usually heartbreak, literal and figurative. In Ovid's *Metamorphoses*, Cupid shoots Apollo with a golden arrow, causing him to fall in love with the nymph Daphne, and then he shoots Daphne with a lead-tipped arrow, causing her to run from Apollo and pray to be turned into a tree. Because her father is the river god Peneus, her prayer is granted.

So did Apollo's heart break into flames,
The sterile fires that feed on empty hopes.

Then Christianity took up the symbol. *The Lord is nigh unto them that are of a broken heart*, reads Psalm 34:18. And in Psalm 69:20: *Reproach hath broken my heart; and I am full of heaviness: and I looked for some to take pity, but there was none; and for comforters, but I found none.* Many seemed to meet their Christian God through the doorway of heartbreak. Saint Augustine, for example, wrote in his *Confessions*:

> *With the arrows of your charity you had pierced our hearts, and we bore your words within us like a sword penetrating us to the core.*

He also wrote that God draws close *only to those whose hearts are crushed.*

From the 884 times that the word *heart* appears in the King James Bible, it's clear the word refers not just to romance but also to the source of one's self. The spirit and all moral and volitional energies. A crushed heart, in other words, is not meant to evoke sentiment. What's at stake is life itself.

IT WAS A THURSDAY. SCOTT WAS AT HOME WITH HIS sister, Megan. The two had spent most days together since school had let out for the summer. Megan was thirteen, Scott was sixteen, and it was Scott's job to look after his younger sister while their parents were at work. Megan loved those early weeks of summer because they were spent with her brother.

The two had just gotten home from getting breakfast when Scott started to leave the house again, and Megan asked him where he was going. Scott said he was heading to the gym and would be back soon. But instead of going to the gym, he walked to a recreational trail nearby, where people biked and took their dogs, and then he waited at the edge of the path where the woods cleared.

Ryan Landers, nine years old, was riding bikes that morning with his mother and twin brother and some family friends. He'd ridden ahead of his mother, and so when he passed Scott on the trail, he was alone. Scott attacked him. He stabbed him with a box cutter in the chest and back. From the defensive wounds on Ryan's body, it's clear he fought back. The fight ended when Scott slit Ryan's throat.

Then Scott got up and left Ryan's body and crossed the path and walked through the woods until he came upon some men working on a house. When the men saw the blood on Scott's clothes, they asked him if he was hurt. He told them to call 911. He told them he'd just stabbed someone. When they asked him why, he said, *Because he was the first one there.*

Ryan's mother is a doctor. When she discovered her son's

body on the path, she tried to resuscitate him. She gave him CPR and tried to stop the bleeding. Someone called 911, and soon EMTs showed up and took Ryan's body to the hospital—his body, because he was already dead.

The police showed up at the construction site and took Scott to the station. He would never go home again.

That night, reporters started showing up at Scott's family's house. But the story never turned into a sensation, because Louisiana had other news to cover. Forty-two miles off the coast, the BP pipeline was leaking millions of barrels of oil into the ocean. Scott's crime earned local coverage, but the rest of the state barely heard his name. When the worst happens, the notion of luck takes on strange significance. What's lucky when your son murders another mother's son? That there is oil spilling into the ocean.

ONE WAY TO THINK ABOUT HEARTBREAK IS IN TERMS of *before* and *after*. And the problem when life gets broken into *before* and *after* is that the edges of the two pieces are jagged and don't fit back together, so what you're left with is a tear and the space between that the mind keeps trying to make sense of but cannot. There are no clean breaks.

THE DAY AFTER THE MURDER, I STAND ON A BUSY street in Washington, D.C., and hear my mother's voice on the other end of the phone, electric with regret for what she is about to say.

Honey, something's happened.

What happened? I say.

Your cousin Scott, she says. *He's had a break.*

What do you mean? I ask. The word *break* sounds vague and antiquated, like *vapors* or *verklempt*.

A psychotic break, she says. *He's killed a little boy.*

I stop walking. I feel suddenly cold in the heat, and I wave my boyfriend on—we'd been walking with a group of people to watch the World Cup on a big screen in Dupont Circle. *I'll catch up with you later,* I whisper. I can't do this with another person looking on or waiting.

Who? I say into the phone. *Who did he kill?*

A stranger, she says. *No one he knew. A nine-year-old boy riding his bike.*

How? My mouth feels dry.

She pauses and then says, *I think he used a knife, some kind of knife.*

Scott is sixteen. I'm twenty-five and have just finished my first year of law school. A year full of stories about accidents and crimes. Sometimes the stories were cases and sometimes they were made-up hypos (short for *hypotheticals*), or fact patterns, that the professor would spin off as an exercise in deductive reasoning. From a specific set of facts, sometimes grisly, sometimes mundane, we were meant to deduce and apply a general rule of law. I'd learned to look for facts that lit up with significance in a story about a contract, a nuisance, a betrayal. I'd tried to shut down the part of me that thought mostly of the characters in the story who'd just lost everything or had everything to lose at the mercy of the law. But I wasn't very good at it, this zeroing in on facts. And here again, on the phone with my mother, I falter. As I scan the facts she has given me—bike path, boy, psychotic break, knife—I can't arrange them in any shape that makes sense.

Murderer. I'm felled by the moral confusion of the word. Scott is my cousin, but in this moment my stomach turns for what he's taken—a life, a child—and I can tell this surprises my mother, whose loyalties are quick to fall in line.

We're going to send money, she says, *to help pay for the defense attorney. Will you, too?*

I don't know, I say. *Can I think about it?*

I guess so, she says. *But I already told them you would.*

I hear the disappointment in her voice, which makes me feel defensive, and in defense I retreat to what I know of justice, no more than the principle of just deserts. In this moment I don't see why Scott deserves our help. It seems to me that the people who need help are the parents of the boy Scott killed, a family I'm certain has been shattered.

Which is to say, after a year of law school, I didn't understand justice. I didn't know anything about its life cycle or force in the three-dimensional world of light and shadows, hearts and heartbreak. Where I saw victim and perpetrator, my mother saw two children. Where I saw a family whose son had been taken, she saw two families. I was not yet a mother. I didn't understand that this was a story about two sons. A story, on both sides, about losing your child, a primal story of pain. And I didn't understand that both boys had fallen prey—one to the violence of murder, and the other to a slow and steady violence, the invisible invasion of disease, ravaging for days and months, maybe years.

Silence fills the space between us on the phone, between what my mother understands about this story and what I don't, and I stand on the sidewalk as the heat takes no prisoners and a group of boys runs past me in their jewel-toned soccer jerseys, sweaty and shouting.

A STONE DROPS INTO WATER AND THE CIRCLES RIPPLE out toward infinity.

I wasn't close to Scott or his father, Abe, who was my first cousin but a couple of decades older than me. Growing up, I'd seen them only a handful of times, mostly at funerals in Alabama, where my father's side of the family is from. So I agreed to send money along with my parents, to help hire an attorney for Scott, and I thought that money might absolve me from further obligation. I resolved to move on, untroubled.

But then at night, when I closed my eyes, I saw a wooded bike path, blood.

Maggie Nelson, who wrote about her aunt's murder and trial, calls this phenomenon *murder mind*:

> *I could work all day on my project with a certain distance, blithely looking up "bullet" or "skull" in my*

rhyming dictionary. But in bed at night I found a smattering of sickening images of violent acts ready and waiting for me.

I tried to turn it off. I tried to be someone who didn't think so much, normal and untroubled. I didn't want this to be a story in which I knew the main characters. I didn't want this story in my family.

Resistance is a rich soil for disorder. *These images coursed through my mind at random intervals*, Nelson writes, *but always with the slapping, prehensile force of the return of the repressed.*

Most everything I knew of Scott before the murder, I knew through my aunt Louise, my father's older sister. My father loved Louise—she was his only ally in a family of *terrorists*, a word he uses to describe his mother, father, and brothers.

Scott was Louise's first grandchild, and she loved him fiercely. I knew his face from the pictures I saw on the walls and side tables of Louise's midwestern house. As a teenager, he looked a bit like his father and a bit like mine. He had a strong jaw and a Roman nose, and his brown curls fell around his face like my father's used to in the seventies, when he was a hippie in Santa Cruz. I knew only a little about Scott's interests (soccer, the FBI) and his achievements at school. I knew he was a good student and that he seemed like a thoughtful person.

On the day of the murder, Aunt Louise called my father, and when he picked up the phone he heard her crying. *Dennis?* she said, and he said, *What's happened? Are you all right?* And between sobs she said, *No, I'm not all right, Scott killed a little boy.*

My father loves Louise, and I do, too. I now understand that Louise was the reason my parents sent money to help pay for Scott's attorney. They felt the vibrations of her pain in their own hearts, a chief liability of love. They were desperate to help her. And though we were far away, the bonds between Louise and my father and my father and me and me and Louise—these made it all feel closer, as if the bonds were chutes, down which panic streamed.

My mind kept turning to Ryan, the boy Scott killed, the space that used to be his life. Tennis shoes by the door, a half-drawn picture. His family's alluvial grief. Ryan was the center, the loss. He was innocent and Scott was guilty. Nothing I'd learned during the first year of law school helped me see beyond these facts, and I couldn't figure out how to consider Scott's guilt without recoiling. But thinking of Ryan made me feel like a traitor, like I was sitting on the wrong side of the aisle.

Maybe the desire to pick a side reflects age-old tribalism. But the instinct I felt was also more modern in its origin, a value of the adversarial legal system I'd spent the previous nine months learning about.

That summer I was living in D.C., working as a legal intern with the Senate Judiciary Committee. It was the summer of Elena Kagan's Supreme Court nomination hearings, and in the days leading up to the hearings, I spent my time poring over hundreds of pages of documents and emails, looking for anything potentially objectionable—a swear word, an unkind remark, a mistake—so that we might be prepared. It was always a time crunch. The White House dropped off boxes and boxes of documents at the end of the day on a Friday and we'd all groan and someone would order pizza. Secretly I was happy for the work. My worst enemies were an unoccupied mind and time alone. I lived by myself then, walked alone to and from work. And when I left the Senate basement in the late evenings, I felt myself drift toward the murder. Walking across the street or stepping off the platform onto the train, an image would flash open: Bloodstained T-shirt. Nine-year-old's bike. The detritus of a bad dream without the reassurance that it's only a dream. My body reacted to these images as if I'd just heard an alarm ringing. I felt a twist in my stomach; my heartbeat sped up.

That summer was unusually hot, even for D.C., with temperatures above a hundred for days at a time. Because I lived on the other side of the city, near the zoo, my commute to and from work took about an hour each way. I committed myself to distraction. On the train, I'd read or listen to

Robert Earl Keen on my headphones as he sang about going home. I focused on people's faces as I climbed the stairs from the underground metro stop toward the dark blue sky of almost night—uniformed workers heading home, a mom carrying her son's backpack while he walked distractedly behind her, friends making plans. The shortcut to my apartment was a foot-worn path through a park, a grassy expanse broken up by two basketball courts, a jungle gym with swings, a fenced-in dog run.

One night just before dusk settled in, something happened as I walked across the park: I looked down at the ground and saw blood. Blood covering the grass, wet, dark blood soaking into the dirt as on a battlefield. I felt panic rise like sickness, but I didn't stop walking. I blinked hard, and when I opened my eyes again, everything was back to normal: the smell of fresh-cut grass, the noise of a pickup game, the familiar trickle of sweat down my spine.

That was a Thursday. Two days later, on Saturday morning, it happened again. I was walking across the same park on my way to meet a friend. It was bright and sunny. A woman was heading toward me—I don't remember anything about her except that she was pushing a stroller with a baby in it. And when she got closer and I looked down at the baby in the stroller, I saw that he was dead. Dark circles under the baby's eyes, his throat bloodied, his head lolling to one side. Dread spread over the park. I looked away and saw a dog, off his leash, whose jaws were red with blood. It was clear, in the logic of the delusion, that the dog had killed the baby.

All of it lasted no more than three seconds, and underneath there was another logic, stable and steady, that told me none of it was real, and that reestablished itself as singular when I concentrated on the heat of the sun on my bare arms.

Jung wrote that *when an inner situation is not made conscious, it happens outside.* The *prehensile force of the return of the repressed.* I was embarrassed, more than a little worried. What did these episodes mean? Nothing, I told myself. Would they continue? I decided they would not.

Twenty-five is the average age of onset for women who develop schizophrenia. At that point, we didn't know if Scott had schizophrenia, but it was the word that had been floating around since his arrest weeks earlier. It did feel like I was balancing on an edge I didn't want to fall over. So I pulled back quickly. As the descendant of Southern women and alcoholics, I excelled at denial. I didn't tell anyone about the episodes. I shoved it all back into the attic of my mind and slammed the door shut.

And I began to pray, a last resort. I picked up a constant prayer, a worrying of words in my mind, over and over, until the words became like stones smoothed by years of touch or tides.

Lord Jesus Christ, have mercy on me. This is the Jesus

prayer, the prayer I started saying to fill any spaces in the day—waking up, walking, riding the train, going to sleep. Part distraction, part defense.

Though I'd grown up going to an Episcopal church with my family, when I was young, I asked my mother if I could stop because I didn't like asking for forgiveness. I couldn't figure out what I'd done wrong. The act of asking felt phony but also unfair. Of course I had made mistakes and made up stories, but I didn't feel that I had *sinned*. I felt too young for sin. She said she understood and didn't make me go except for holidays.

But the Jesus prayer didn't come to me from childhood or church. I found it in Salinger's *Franny & Zooey*, which I read for the first time in high school. Franny picks it up from a book about a Russian pilgrim who wants to know what it means in the Bible when it says we ought to pray without ceasing. The pilgrim goes on a journey to find out, speaking with different spiritual teachers along the way. In the end, he finds himself repeating the Jesus prayer over and over, quietly, until it becomes unconscious, involuntary, synced to the rhythm of his steps and heartbeat and breath.

Lord Jesus Christ, have mercy on me. Lord Jesus Christ, have mercy on me.

Depending on how quickly I said the words, I'd say it all on the inbreath and then over again on the outbreath, or I'd break it into two parts, *Lord Jesus Christ* on the inhale, *have mercy on me* on the exhale. After a week or so, I found a quieting in the repetition. Murder mind wasn't gone completely, but the stress was less acute—a kind of unhaunting. And this felt like mercy. Which is to say, I got what I'd been asking for hundreds of times a day, if not from Jesus himself then in the asking. The poet Fanny Howe writes that God *exists as the witness of what is and also as light and energy, neither of which can be touched except by touching itself.*

But there is something else, too: what happened to Ryan, what Scott did, and what happened to his brain—the word it raised, in spite of myself, was *evil*. Other members of my family felt this way, too. Whisperings of evil trickled down. My father started wearing a small cross around his neck, tucked into his shirt. When I talked to him about the feeling of evil, we always lowered our voices, as if someone might hear us. It was embarrassing to say it, and it didn't make any sense, so we whispered. Sometimes I had the feeling that talking about evil might summon something impossible to put back in its box. Which is to say, I prayed not only for distraction and relief but also because prayer felt like the apposite lexicon.

SOMETIMES AN INDIVIDUAL WORD ENACTS A SCENE. The word *heartbreak* paints, in its compound structure, physical pain. Death is the literal outcome of a heart that breaks. And the truth of this enactment finds proof in the body and modern neuroscience. In 2011, researchers at the

University of Michigan used an fMRI machine to show that the same parts of our brain light up in heartbreak (participants had just gone through a breakup with someone they loved) as when we are burned by a hot probe.

The reason for this, they believe, is evolutionary. In the prehistoric forests of our forebearers, being alone meant death. You needed family, a tribe, a band to rove and hunt with, in order to survive. So we evolved to feel the pain of separation, isolation, loneliness—and the experiences that lead us there, like unrequited love or the death of a partner—as a life-or-death proposition.

Which is to say, when you think of your worst-case scenario in the middle of the night, your most feared heartbreak, and you think you might not make it through—when you pray to a God you're not sure you believe in to be spared, when you ask for mercy—you're listening to the wisdom of a memory that's fifty-two million years old.

WHO CAN OFFER MERCY? PEOPLE, SYSTEMS, GODS. Our own selves to our own selves. There was a time when I found a good deal of mercy in alcohol and pills. Prayer and sitting still are less immediate in offering relief than that, but after a while, what they offer seems to last longer.

Before I began reciting the Jesus prayer, mercy was a thing I wasn't sure Scott deserved. I couldn't see past the harm he'd done. I couldn't see past Ryan. What I didn't understand then is that no one deserves mercy, and that is its whole point. As

Bryan Stevenson writes in his book *Just Mercy*, *Mercy belongs to the undeserving.* For those who are guilty, in debt for what they took, what's *deserved* is punishment—the forfeiture of freedom. A life for a life. But mercy transcends any notion of desert and offers something new.

And if no one deserves mercy, you might say that everyone deserves it, the line between *no one* and *everyone*, nothing and everything, confused when you bend the line into a circle and the two ends meet at the top. *Go and learn what this means: "I desire mercy, not sacrifice,"* Jesus tells the Pharisees in Matthew.

It was only after I had started asking for mercy and began to feel its quiet in my own small life that I began wanting it for Scott. I don't believe this was a coincidence. Nor was it a decision. Something moved without my moving it; something was made clear.

AT THE SAME TIME I PICKED UP THE JESUS PRAYER, Aunt Louise was losing the lifeline of her own prayers. Louise, who had gone to church every Sunday for decades, who'd sat through Bible groups and prayer circles and cooked for fellowship gatherings, could no longer talk to God or feel the comfort that this talking offered. She had loved Scott with her whole heart. He was her first grandson. *The one you didn't have to worry about*, she told me. This is something I'll hear a lot from Aunt Louise over the years.

I didn't know much else about him. After the murder,

two facts attached to his name like an epithet in a Greek myth: he was the captain of the varsity soccer team and had a 4.0 GPA. I found myself repeating these facts as I'd heard them. But later I found out that neither one was true, exactly, both exaggerations. Scott did play varsity soccer, but he wasn't the captain, and he made good grades, but not perfect grades. I see now how this exaggeration was meant to telegraph the break between *before* and *after*, that severe incongruence. The unforeseeability of what happened felt more extreme than the facts alone conveyed, so somewhere along the chain of storytelling the facts were amplified to match the feeling.

I wanted to learn more. One night, a few years after Scott's arrest, when I was visiting Aunt Louise in Illinois, I asked her what Scott was like, *Before*, I said, and she knew what I meant. We were sitting on the plaid couch of her suburban ranch home, while Uncle Jerry watched TV loud enough for the whole neighborhood to hear.

He was polite and easygoing, she said. *Considerate and kind. He talked about college, his plans for the future. He went to church, he did the things his parents asked him to do around the house. He was the one you didn't have to worry about.* And then, after a long pause, she opened her eyes wide and shook her head a little and said, *He was beloved. He was beloved.* Her eyes filled with tears, and she sighed and looked away.

Once I spoke with a psychologist who said that grief is

the form love takes when what's loved is lost. It's love's extension into absence. Scott isn't gone, not the way Ryan is. But for those who loved him, some days he may as well be. Some days it would be easier if he were. What happens to the love that rushes out to him from Louise? It turns into something if not harder than grief—because who can measure the relative hardship of heartbreak?—then certainly more gnarled. For Louise, the murder was a severing, and when she was alone and tried to turn to God, the severing meant silence.

That night I heard her heartbreak, which was also a testimony to shock, to the fact of unforeseeability. Sometimes my father will shake his head and say what happened is a nightmare, but that isn't quite right because what happened no one could have dreamed.

I FELT MYSELF HOPING AND WAITING FOR A DIAGNOSIS (not for any legal reason—it had not yet occurred to me that a court might find him sane), but because I thought that it would settle the why. If Scott were sick, Aunt Louise would have a one-word explanation. A phrase to contain the uncontainable. Without a diagnosis, she'd have to face the idea that her beloved grandson had committed an act that felt evil without explanation.

A few days after the arrest, Louise had told my father, who'd told me, that Scott had told the police he'd given in to the voices. That was why everyone assumed schizophrenia.

Schizophrenia would organize the possibilities for what might happen next.

But in the weeks after his arrest, no diagnosis came. At first I thought the delay was a matter of crossed wires. I imagined information scribbled down on a doctor's notepad during an evaluation in a dire, over-air-conditioned room, passed on to Abe and then to Louise and then to my father and then to me, the facts changing or dropping away with each subsequent phone call.

But then we learned that the silence we heard reflected the silence there was. Scott hadn't been diagnosed.

In July, a month after the murder, he pled not guilty by reason of insanity at an arraignment hearing. This was reassuring. No diagnosis yet, but surely one would come now. A month after that, in August, the Senate confirmed Justice Kagan in an uncontroversial vote by today's standards.

Time was moving forward.

After the confirmation hearings were over, I sent three books to the county jail, because reading was all Scott could do. The jail required the books to be new, sent directly from a vendor with a receipt. I wasn't sure what a sixteen-year-old boy might want to read, so I thought back to my brother's bookshelf and the soliloquies about Márquez and Hemingway I'd heard for years from past boyfriends. I decided on *For Whom the Bell Tolls*, *A River Runs Through It*, and *One Hundred Years of Solitude*. The sadness in these books didn't strike me when I sent them. The sadness, and the particular violence (war, murder, being devoured by ants) imagined by each writer. Now I see how each narrative swirls toward loss, but sadness wasn't what I was going for. I was going for escape, the gate that swings open when a sentence follows another sentence and another and suddenly you're somewhere else, and the world is new. I was after beauty, sweep. That those guideposts led me to stories about loss now seems inevitable.

So much can go unaccounted for in life. Why did I send books then? Sending books seemed like a small way to ease the pain I imagined Scott was feeling. I wanted to help if I could, which was an honest instinct but also rooted in an inability to be still amid the rubble. There was so much that had been broken when Scott murdered Ryan, and I was desperate to do something remedial, however small. Reading was always the way I had found sense and beauty in a world that made no sense. Books were reliable when people weren't. That was what I wanted to give Scott. James Baldwin wrote:

> You think your pain and your heartbreak are unprecedented in the history of the world, but then you read. It was Dostoevsky and Dickens who taught me that the things that tormented me most were the very things that connected me with all the people who were alive, who had ever been alive.

But sending books also represented the beginning of a crossing over. I was moving into a territory that would thereafter be a part of my world, a territory I have had to find a way to claim.

Recently at a dinner party, a woman I didn't know asked me why I *cared*. About Scott, she meant. Scott had come up because someone had asked what I was writing about and I scuttled through a vague sketch, hoping to deter any follow-up questions. I was not prepared for the woman's bluntness, and I had no good answer to her question. It felt that I was being asked to account for something intangible, unknowable, but also self-evident. I wanted to say, How could I not care? Wouldn't you have cared, too? Wouldn't you have sent books? But of course the answer is no. She wouldn't have, and that was why she was asking. It's not a moral difference, but it's a space that asks to be crossed in the telling, in the writing.

The meditation teacher Jack Kornfield sometimes tells a Russian folk story in his dharma talks about Baba Yaga, an old woman with *a wild, haglike visage who stirs her pot and knows all things*. Baba Yaga lives deep in the forest, and people who set out to find her and learn their fortunes are made *to go into the dark, to ask dangerous questions*. In the story, there are three seekers. When the first seeker knocks on her door, she opens it and asks, *Are you on your own errand or are you sent by another?* The young man answers, *I am sent by my father*, at which point Baba Yaga throws him into her pot and cooks him. The second seeker is a young woman. When Baba Yaga asks her the same question, *Are you on your own errand or are you sent by another*, she answers, *I am on my own errand*. Baba Yaga throws her in the pot and cooks her, too. The third seeker, another young woman, *deeply confused by the world*, sees the smoke from Baba Yaga's fire and knows it's dangerous. When Baba Yaga asks her, *Are you on your own errand, or are you sent by another*, the young woman answers truly:

> "In large part I'm on my own errand, but in large part I also come because of others. And in large part I have come because you are here, and because of the forest, and something I have forgotten, and in large part I know not why I come." Baba Yaga regards her for a moment and says, "You'll do," and shows her into the hut.

I don't know why I crossed over into caring about Scott. But my answers to the question have, over the years, sounded like all three of the characters' answers in the story. The unfortunates who got thrown into the pot and the last woman who's spared. The last one is the truest, and what I might have said to the woman at the dinner if I'd had my wits about me and the courage—

In large part I was on my own errand, but in large part

I also cared because of others. And in large part I crossed over because he was there, and because of the forest, and something I had forgotten, and in large part I know not why.

I can't name all the reasons I crossed over and started caring, but I do know why I care now: it's hard not to care about someone when you begin to know him.

AT FIRST MY PARENTS WERE AFRAID THAT SCOTT WOULD be executed. When my mother mentioned this one night on the phone, I told her it wasn't possible. The Supreme Court had banned the death penalty for anyone under eighteen in *Roper v. Simmons* (2005). I remembered reading *Roper* in Crim (Criminal Law class) the fall before—those *evolving standards of decency*—and this made me remember the box of textbooks and notebooks I'd lugged across the country with me, in case I'd need to look something up during my internship, which of course I hadn't.

I walked across the hot living room into the hotter bedroom and found the box. I dug out the heavy red textbook with gold lettering across a black banner. I opened it and scanned the pages until I found the elements of murder: *The statutory elements for murder are the* actus reus *(guilty act) and the* mens rea *(guilty mind). Both are required.*

There was no question about the *actus reus* in Scott's case. He'd confessed the act immediately when he walked off the bike path and through the woods and told the carpenters to call the police. But if he really had suffered a break, how would this break affect the *mens rea*? In Louisiana state law, the *mens rea* component of murder is codified as the *specific intent to kill or to inflict great bodily harm*. Could someone suffering from some kind of psychosis be capable of intent?

I picked up a spiral-bound notebook from the box, the black one I'd used for Crim, and flipped through until I saw *JUVENILE JUSTICE*. There were my notes on *Roper*:*

- *ROPER V. SIMMONS* (2005): Redraws lines at 18. Overturns *Stanford*,† which drew line at fifteen.

- FACTS: Christopher Simmons (17) broke into Shirley Crook's home with his friend, with the idea to rob

---

* One interesting thing about *Roper*: it was one of the first cases to feature the science of how immature an eighteen-year-old brain is and how much brains continue to change throughout our twenties, research that is still evolving today. But what was clear enough then is that the final part of the brain to mature is the prefrontal cortex, which is the center for impulse control and moral reasoning. When Christopher Simmons was interviewed by a local newspaper about why he murdered Shirley Crook, he said, *I ask myself why, and I don't understand why. We just lost all sense of stealing things.*

Like Scott, Simmons was not an especially sympathetic defendant—the crime was planned, and therefore, in a legal sense, cold-blooded. Unlike Scott, his personal history offered a narrative of abuse that might have amounted to *mitigating evidence*. Mitigating evidence, or extenuating circumstances, cannot be used to acquit a defendant, but can have the power to affect sentencing. Yet Simmons's original counsel did not offer salient details about his past—how he'd been physically and verbally abused as a child, and by the time of the murder, how he was a regular drinker and pot smoker—because they feared them to be more condemning than helpful.

† *Stanford v. Kentucky* (1989): Holding that although it might not be okay

and murder her. Burglary only netted six dollars but they went through with the murder, blindfolding and tying up and throwing her off bridge. Cause of death was drowning. Simmons sentenced to die by jury in Missouri. Appealed sentence up to Supreme Court.

- MAJORITY: relied on same *evolving standards of decency test* as in *Thompson*. Asks: have we changed enough as a society to justify overturning old laws? Court said yes.

Because *Roper* took death off the table, the next harshest sentence available to prosecutors in Scott's case would be life without parole (LWOP).

I sat down on the bed and opened my computer. Outside the sun was setting. A fire engine howled. I looked up LWOP

---

to execute a fifteen-year-old, it *is* okay to execute a sixteen-, seventeen-, or eighteen-year-old. Kevin Stanford (seventeen years old at the time of his crime) was tried as an adult and sentenced to death for raping and murdering Barbel Poore, a gas station attendant and new mother. Justice Antonin Scalia, who wrote the majority opinion, pointed to the lack of settled consensus among the fifty states as to the unconstitutionality of executing a teenager. And even if there was consensus, he wrote, that isn't the appropriate inquiry. What matters is what the Founding Fathers imagined when they wrote the Eighth Amendment, not how we interpret that amendment today. In other words: originalism vs. living Constitution.

In terms of mitigating evidence, according to a later petition by his attorneys to commute his sentence, Kevin Stanford was neglected, beaten, and sexually abused by his family and community. By the time of his arrest for rape and murder, he had been trading sex for money and drugs for years. Stanford was also Black, whereas Christopher Simmons was white, which should not be ignored given the way the Court decided these two cases.

for juveniles. *Graham v. Florida* popped up, which was decided just a month before Scott's crime. On the bottom of the page from my Crim notebook, under *Roper*, I added:

- GRAHAM V. FLORIDA (2010): banned life without parole (LWOP) sentences for juveniles convicted of <u>nonhomicide</u> crimes.

- KENNEDY (MAJORITY): the juvenile should not be deprived of the opportunity to achieve maturity of judgment and self-recognition of <u>human worth and potential.</u>

The case didn't apply to Scott—it was narrowed to all crimes less than homicide. But the word *potential* struck me as vital. The essence of what it means, or should mean, to be sixteen years old, no matter what else had come before. I thought it might point toward a sea change. An evolving understanding that might open a way for Scott to get something less than LWOP. I thought there might be hope.

Some people serving time talk about hope as a necessity, and some describe it as a luxury. The families of people in prison divide down a similar line. In my own family, hope seemed like a risk no one was taking. No one claimed it amid the details of Scott's crime.

The sky was losing light. The crickets were picking up where the traffic left off. I looked up sentencing trends in

Louisiana. I was trying to get a sense of what was likely. I learned that Louisiana was one of three states, along with Michigan and Pennsylvania, that accounts for over two-thirds of all juvenile LWOP sentences in the country. I read that in the past year, there were only six cases of diversion—a mechanism of the court system in which a young offender is diverted away from the traditional court system into a treatment program or a specialty court, like a drug court.

How can you hope for mercy in a system that likens mercy to weakness? I learned that night that Scott's only chance would be the insanity defense, which required a legally recognizable diagnosis. *Let it be schizophrenia*, I thought. *Let there be a diagnosis.* The poet and writer Anne Boyer describes *diagnosis* as *the mercy of a name*.

GRIEF IS NOT A DIAGNOSIS, BUT A PLACE, OR A STATE. A natural state, like sleep or love, which can also function as an explanation. *I didn't hear you, I was asleep. I couldn't make it, I was grieving.*

But a grief that gets stuck is diagnosable. The clinical term for *stuck* is *complicated grief*, or *prolonged grief disorder*.

This is one of the first things that Dr. Bonnie Gorscak tries to explain to her patients—the idea that grief is natural. I spoke to her one day on the phone, years ago, after I'd started to learn about heartbreak and was reading about the Center for Complicated Grief, where Gorscak is a trainer and supervisor. At the center, founded by Dr. Katherine Shear and housed at Columbia University, they understand grief as love's extension after loss, i.e., nothing to get over. Grief goes on and on and changes just like our love for the living, if we're lucky.

Complicated grief is complicated because it doesn't change shape or size; it stays unlivable. But mostly, Dr. Gorscak tells me, people tend to underestimate how "well" they'll do in grief. Our body and heart and brain were built for this, she says. We're evolutionarily wired to survive it, despite our instincts telling us otherwise.

When I asked her about heartbreak, she said she doesn't use the word clinically but her patients use it regularly as a way to describe themselves. *Heartbroken, brokenhearted.* Other common descriptions of grief involve a missing or broken limb, a constant pain, a crushing weight.

When she thinks of heartbreak, she says, what strikes her is the way it can be an experience of compassion, how our hearts can break for others. This makes me think of a Chinese word I'd read about, *xīnténg* (心疼), whose literal translation is *heart aches* but whose meaning pertains to the specific pain of witnessing. A kind of physical empathy. How my father felt his sister's ache in his own heart when she called to tell him about Scott.

Dr. Gorscak recalls, out loud, the times she's felt it come up inside the details of her own life. The first was many years prior, with an ill family member. Faced with terminal cancer, her loved one would often talk about the future *without a shadow of sadness*. In these moments, the feeling that came up for her, and the word to describe it, was *heartbreaking*. The other instance was a betrayal, when a trusted friend let her down in a way she couldn't have imagined. *I am struck by how different each of these experiences are*, she said.

> *And yet heartbreak is somehow involved in both. The first one is a little more along the lines of what we've been discussing today—the compassion focus, but the second one is so different from that. It is a sort of loss, as you were saying, but more along the lines of loss of trust, disillusionment, disappointment, loss of innocence. As I think about it, there are some sort of grief-like emotions involved in each.*

Because I'm not a scientist or clinician, I have not taken it upon myself to parse the difference between heartbreak and grief. These definitions were something I wanted to get right in the beginning, but over time the effort felt forced and irrelevant. What I know is that heartbreak, as a word, is more vast than grief; it holds more and runs along a wider spectrum of possibility, from very big to very small. But like grief, heartbreak can be complicated. It often is. Heartbreak can be a moment—a discrete event, a notch along a timeline—or a slow, protracted breaking. It can be a state, like grief, like love, that goes on and on. If all goes well, it changes.

In another study, neuroscientists compared the brains of people in love to the brains of people in heartbreak. To study heartbroken subjects, the scientists put out a call for people recently rejected (and *in such bad shape*, as Helen Fisher, one of the researchers, put it in her TED Talk). Other requirements, according to the text of the study, were "thinking about rejecter at least 85 percent of the time," as well as a "lack of emotional control," such as "inappropriate phoning, writing or e-mailing, pleading for reconciliation, sobbing for hours, drinking too much and/or making dramatic entrances and exits into the rejecter's home, place of work or social space to express anger, despair or passionate love."

They put up the notice on a college campus and got plenty of respondents. To study love, they looked at the brains of people in new relationships as well as those of longtime married couples. All subjects got sent through the fMRI machine, while being shown photos of their lovers and asked questions meant to prod memories. They found that in the heartbroken brain and the brain in love, the ventral tegmental area (VTA), a part of the core, reptilian brain, was particularly activated. The VTA governs everything underneath thinking or feeling. The reptilian brain tells us what we need and how to get it, how to keep it. When Dr. Gorscak says that grief is the form love takes after loss, it's not only a nice idea. It's also how the brain reflects these physiological states. The emotions are distinct, but the primal need remains. Heartbreak is love when the story changes, when you turn the page.

MY FATHER WROTE TO TELL ME THAT THE BOOKS I sent had arrived at the jail. He also said he'd heard that the judge had appointed the state's doctors to the case. What did that mean? he asked. I wasn't sure, so I asked a friend who was working at a DA's office for the summer.

The first order of business, she said, was to figure out if Scott was fit to stand trial. Answering this question requires the defense and prosecution to hire their own experts. Then the question is whether these two sets of experts will agree. They rarely do. One of the main points of experts in the criminal justice system, aside from their expertise, is that they're supposed to be impartial. But if they're impartial it bears asking why there needs to be two different sets. In any case, all this can take a long time. Mostly the machinery of justice moves slowly.

And here's what can't be overstated: one half of this machine was pitted against Scott, was not interested in finding out what had happened to his brain and how to treat it, because such an inquiry would be purportedly against the interests of Scott's victim, Ryan, whose voice could no longer convey his interests because it had been silenced. Because Scott had silenced it. Because Scott had killed him.

I am trying to avoid euphemisms and the passive voice. Maggie Nelson writes:

> *Perhaps because I have spent hours sermonizing to students about the sins of the passive voice—how it can obfuscate meaning, deaden vitality, and abandon the task of assigning agency or responsibility—I find the grammar of justice maddening. It's always "rendered," "served," or "done."*

For me, euphemisms arise not only because of the system's passive obfuscation, and not only because of squeamishness, but also because the split between the person who committed this murder and the person Scott was before, and is now, feels stark. In some meaningful way, it was not *he* who did this; it was a sickness, a broken brain.

But legally it was him. His name, his social security number. So Scott continued to wait in a county jail, without services or treatment, while a group of experts examined him for the purposes of a courtroom's artifice of truth telling. We waited, too. If my father or I asked Aunt Louise about a diagnosis, she always reiterated—as if it were sufficient, as if we were crazy for having forgotten—that it had been a *psychotic break*. I didn't know then that these were the only words we'd ever have.

ON A HOT DAY IN JUNE, ALMOST EXACTLY FIVE YEARS after Scott killed Ryan, Dylann Roof murdered nine congregants of Emanuel African Methodist Episcopal Church in Charleston, South Carolina: Reverend Clementa Pinckney, Tywanza Sanders, Cynthia Hurd, Sharonda Coleman-Singleton, Myra Thompson, Ethel Lance, Daniel Simmons, DePayne Middleton-Doctor, and Susie Jackson.

When I first read headlines about the attack and saw Roof's mug shot, I thought of Scott's. Then I thought of Adam Lanza's picture, his sunken cheeks and hollow eyes. Aside from being murderers, they were not especially alike, these boys. Scott's crime wasn't a mass murder like theirs, and it wasn't racially motivated, like Roof's. But I heard an echo among them. For one thing, each act felt shocking and unforeseeable once it was made real. Despite Roof's white supremacist animus, which he was open about and which he'd been nursing for years, the scale of the massacre was shocking to everyone, even to himself. As *The New York Times* reported: *[Roof] expressed surprise when the agents told him how many had been killed. "I wouldn't believe you," he said after one first suggested that nine people had died. "There wasn't even nine people there. Are you guys lying to me?"*

But most of all, I heard the echo because each was young and white and each had turned his pain or sickness into a weapon. (Is it wrong to assign, linguistically and factually, that kind of agency? Or is it worse to strip away all agency by herding them under the umbrella of mental illness?) There was some dark matter that connected them in my mind.

And then I read about Roof's penalty trial, the part where the judge decides the defendant's sentence, during which Dylann Roof's mother had a cardiac event. Rachel Kaadzi Ghansah, who wrote a Pulitzer Prize–winning piece for *GQ* about Dylann Roof called "A Most American Terrorist," was at the trial:

> *I was seated directly behind Dylann Roof's mother, and because she is skin and bones, it was apparent that she was having some kind of fit. She trembled and shook until her knees buckled and she slid slowly onto the bench, mouth agape, barely moving. She said, over and over again, "I'm sorry. I'm so sorry." She seemed to be speaking to her boyfriend, but maybe it was meant for Felicia Sanders, who was soon to take the stand. A communiqué that was a part of the bond that mothers have, one that was brought up by the radiant shame one must feel when your son has wreaked unforgivable havoc on another mother's child.*

On the day of the shooting, Felicia Sanders hid under a table with her granddaughter, playing dead, as she heard her son, Tywanza, pleading with Roof. *We mean you no harm*, he said. Sanders had to watch her son bleed to death, silent for the sake of her granddaughter's life.

Roof's attorney tried to use Roof's mother's attack in their appeal for a mistrial, citing it as evidence of overly gruesome and emotional testimony that would prejudice the jury. The appeal was denied. And Dylann Roof's mother survived her attack following a brief stay at the hospital. Shortly after, it started being reported that her diagnosis was Takotsubo cardiomyopathy, or broken heart syndrome.

Takotsubo means *octopus trap*. A heart suffering from Takotsubo cardiomyopathy looks caught and constricted, like an octopus, with its upper chambers ballooning as if trying to escape. Over 90 percent of cases occur in women over the age of fifty—doctors aren't sure why—and though most patients recover from broken heart syndrome, it can be fatal. Researchers at Harvard believe it to be vastly underdiagnosed in the United States, mostly missed by doctors looking for signs of heart attack, which more regularly present in men. In *Heart: A History*, the cardiologist Sandeep Jauhar writes:

> *In the early part of the twentieth century, Karl Pearson, a biostatistician studying cemetery headstones, noticed that husbands and wives tend to die within a year of each other. This finding supports what we now know to be true: heartbreak can cause heart attacks.*

The notion that heartbreak can cause physical damage to the heart has long been a trope of narrative. Ten of Shakespeare's characters die from heart failure incited by grief or shock, including Enobarbus, in *Antony and Cleoptra*, who wills his heart to break in a fit of guilt after deserting Antony (*Throw my heart / Against the flint and hardness of my fault, / Which, being dried with grief, will break to powder, / And finish all foul thoughts*); Falstaff, in *Henry V*, who dies from rejection (*The King has killed his heart*); and King Lear, following his daughter Cordelia's death, whose last words in the quarto version of the play are directed to his heart (*Break . . . prithee break*).*

But it was not only playwrights and poets who accepted the metaphorical heart's effect on the physical heart. Medical writings from the Elizabethan period urged against "sores of the soule," because it was believed that they could stop the heart, noting sadness's high rate of mortality. Which is to say, Takotsubo cardiomyopathy is a new name for an old occurrence.

I PACKED MY BIG SUITCASE AND SHIPPED A BOX OF books back to California. Fall was coming, the second year of law school just about to start. Back in Palo Alto, the

---

* These are not Lear's last lines in the folio version. But the quarto version came first, in 1608. The folio version, which is mostly what we read today, changed some lines around and appeared in 1623, after Shakespeare's death.

palm trees lined the boulevards, and the grass on the hills in the distance had turned brown over a summer without rain. Every few weeks my father called with bad news.

The state is trying him as an adult.

They're not letting him wear his retainer in the jail, his teeth are rearranging.

They're not giving him any treatment or medicine.

He wants to kill himself.

When I decided to go to law school, I'd wanted to learn how to fight injustice. But sitting in Contracts and Civil Procedure during my first year, huge auditoriums full of anxious students jockeying to prove their perspicacity, my desire gave way to doubt. I worried I'd made a big mistake. I worried I wasn't meant to be where I was.

On the drive across the country before orientation, L and I hit a wild turkey on the way up to Mount Rushmore. We had to pick the blood and feathers out of the front grate. A few days later, the car broke down just outside of Buffalo, Wyoming, population 4,000. There were no rental cars, no taxis, trains, or planes. We paid a man named Rolly $50 to drive us to the nearest airport, in Sheridan. All my things and clothes stayed in the car that sat at an auto shop with a hundred old cars languishing behind it. We couldn't wait for it because classes were starting in a few days. I spent the first month of school wearing the same five shirts.

The day before orientation, L and I sat on Stinson Beach and decided to stay together despite his job and home in D.C.

After we said goodbye and he flew back east, I missed him terribly. We were falling in love then. Sitting in classes that first term, I'd think back to the turkey and the breakdown in Buffalo and wonder if it was a sign.

But by the end of that first year, I had gathered some confidence or clarity about what I was doing and why. Then Scott murdered Ryan. And when I returned to campus in the fall for 2L, it all felt renewedly dissonant. I didn't care about the things I knew I was supposed to care about—law firms, law review, moot court, clerkships. It had something to do with Scott sitting in a jail cell three thousand miles away, his teeth rearranging in his head, as I floated from class to class, my arms full of casebooks, stories of accidents and harms. I was already beginning to doubt the law's adequacy to fix anything that was broken. And the murder drew a line between what was real and what was theater. Law school, along with all its competitions and lunches and anxieties, was theater. In real life, the law made real victims.

In a few months I would find my way off campus and I would find a way to make my education feel real. I would start teaching in a juvenile detention center. I would start representing clients at a pro bono law clinic in East Palo Alto, once dubbed America's "murder capital," a town that represented, like many communities adjacent to elite universities, the other side of wealth concentration. Antonyms for concentration include *lack, dispersal, separation.*

But in the beginning of that fall, I was myself dispersed. I lived off campus, in Los Altos, in a one-room cottage in the backyard of an Israeli family, where lemon and persimmon trees framed the walkway to my front door. Sometimes on Sundays the family would invite me over for pancakes. I always said yes and then wished I hadn't. I was trying to get a grip on things. I signed up for classes in Juvenile Justice, I was turning in my work, I had friends, and I had L and a backyard full of fruit, and I showered every day. But at my worst, when I drove to class in the morning, I thought about pulling the steering wheel into a tree. I thought about how good it could be *not* to be. And when I remember eating pancakes with my landlords on Sundays, I remember the pull of sadness, that persistent undertow.

SOMETIMES AS I DRIVE THE DIRT ROADS AND EMPTY highways of Vermont, where I now live, I'll pass a marker by the road that shows how high the water rose during Hurricane Irene. Often the measuring stick points to a spot above my head. I didn't live here then, but my parents did, and the memory of the disaster persists around the state. Thousands were stranded behind washed-out roads. Many lost their homes. That was 2011.

When scientists at the University of Arkansas did a study of everyone diagnosed with broken heart syndrome in 2011, the highest rate of cases—three times the national average—presented in Vermont. The second-highest rate was in Missouri, where a tornado killed at least 158 people in Joplin. The scientists noted that Vermont and Missouri were not the only states in 2011 that experienced grave natural disasters, but because Irene and the Joplin tornado were unprecedented, the residents of Vermont and Missouri were unprepared, and therefore more vulnerable to suffering.

Which is to say, the broken heart reflects another kind of break—a break in our regularly scheduled programming. You didn't see it coming, and you weren't prepared. Of course, plenty breaks your heart that you did see coming. An addict's masochistic demise, an ill-fated affair, a death that follows diagnosis. But the tragedies we don't see coming seem to shatter with particular force.

Break is a word whose sound suits its meaning, sudden and severe, like the snap of a tree branch. It comes from the old English *brecan*, which carried a connotation of annulment. I've come to think of this etymology in heartbreak, when what you feel is loss but also a betrayal, as if some promise you were made was broken, some contract rendered void. Your heart breaks once and then again for the broken promise no one ever made you, least of all God, on whose flimsy foundation you built your plans and life, so easily washed away.

Which leaves so many holding that impossible question: *Why?* Across all accounts of heartbreak I have read and seen and even felt, it seems particularly hard to let go of *why* when what hits you comes out of the blue. A few recent news headlines:

DEADLY ATTACKS IN ETHIOPIA LEAVE
VICTIMS WONDERING WHY

FAMILY OF EAST TEXAS HOMICIDE
VICTIMS LEFT WONDERING WHY

HUSBAND OF NEBRASKA AVE SHOOTING
VICTIM LEFT WONDERING, "WHY?"

FAMILY OF D.C. MURDER VICTIM
LEFT WONDERING

But there's rarely just one answer to the question why, and it's rarely satisfying. Reasons are like dominos; causes link up like chains.

I first learned about chains of causation during 1L. Our floppy-haired young Torts professor, on loan from Harvard, bounced around the room laying out the facts of a case about a train, and then a case about fire and a gust of wind that blew the fire and I don't remember what else. The point is, it seemed like a game. An intellectual exercise in physics and ethics. *Where do you draw the line?* our professor asked, with a twinkle in his eye.

Legal causation begins with *foreseeability*, a concept pertaining to actions, reactions, and predictability. And technically it's a concept relevant only to tort law, the crimes caused by negligence rather than criminal intent,* where we hold a defendant responsible for his actions *only if* the consequences of those actions were foreseeable. If a reasonable person† could or should have been able to see what could happen when he left the candle burning, the gun unlocked, we hold him accountable. But if the outcomes were unforeseen, too attenuated, or too unexpected, we don't.‡ Some examples of events the law deems unforeseeable include criminal acts of strangers§ that interrupt the chain of causation and *acts of God*, like earthquakes and floods.

---

* In criminal law, the foreseeability of a crime doesn't come up explicitly—it's baked into the requirements of a charge, integral to the *actus reus*. In Scott's case, the act establishing cause was the attack. Ryan's death was the foreseeable consequence of the attack. The exception to this is felony murder trials, where murder is an accidental effect of some other crime, like burglary, rather than the intended outcome. Then foreseeability matters again.

† The Reasonable Person doctrine is a legal fiction that functions as a standard for the courts. *Black's Law Dictionary* defines the Reasonable Man as *an ordinary person who exercises care while avoiding extremes of boldness and carefulness.*

‡ In this way, someone might be factually responsible for something bad happening, but not legally responsible. There are two prongs to legal causation: factual cause and legal cause. Factual cause, or cause-in-fact, deals with mechanics and is established by the but-for test: *But for X, Y wouldn't have happened.* Legal cause, or proximate cause, considers more than mechanics, and answers the sometimes more complicated question of responsibility. This second prong hinges on *foreseeability*.

§ See *Port Auth. v. Arcadian Corp.*, 189 F.3d 305 (3d Cir. 1999) (holding, under both New Jersey and New York law, that manufacturers of fertilizer products could not reasonably foresee that their products would be used in the 1993 World Trade Center terrorist attack).

In Scott's case, does the chain of causation begin inside his brain? In utero? Or in the culture he grew up in? What strand of DNA or ancient trauma might predict the break and how far back would we have to go to find it? Where does the chain of events start that led us here, to the howling center of loss, and what isn't an act of God?

The writer and Freudian analyst-in-training Michael Sendrow, whom I met at a wedding in 2019, posted an essay online called "Secondhand Victims," in which he writes: *In the aftermath of any . . . violence, the desperate impulse to understand why it happened tends to overshadow the grim reality of . . . the tragedy.*

For Scott and Adam Lanza and Dylann Roof, some part of *why* can surely be answered with a diagnosis. But, as Sendrow writes, *[b]laming violence on mental illness reflects our desire for quick fixes.* Plus, *the trajectory of humanity is propelled by violence.* In this way, mental illness becomes a catchall, a kind of scapegoat: *We project our worst impulses onto that sick mind. We see this sick mind not as a condition of any collective illness but instead the cause. This sick mind is the source and expression of society's faults and failures.*

In her piece on Roof, Ghansah traces back a related thread of causation for the Charleston massacre:

> *Dylann Roof was educated in a state whose educational standards from 2011 are full of lesson plans*

*that focus on . . . "the viewpoint of slave owners"
and highlight "the economic necessity of slave
labor." . . . Roof is what happens when we prefer vast
historical erasures to real education about race. . . .
It is possible that Dylann Roof is not an outlier at
all, then, but rather emblematic of an approaching
storm.*

And the prison psychologist James Gilligan writes
that murder is not as senseless as it seems, that men do
not kill for *no reason. Murderers*, he writes, *see themselves as literally having no other choice; to them, it's
"him or me."*

These explanations for violence run together like strands
of a river emptying out into the same sea. They point not
only to the search for sense in the face of violence but also
to the likelihood of sense behind what feels senseless.
Something foreseeable behind what feels unforeseeable. You
cannot prepare yourself for every disaster, every deviation
from the script. But maybe not everything is as shocking or
inexplicable as it feels when your heart is broken and you're
left holding *why*.

That fall I sent three more books to Scott: *Gilead*, *A
Moveable Feast*, and *Lonesome Dove*. I was still trying to
send books that I thought a sixteen-year-old boy might like.
One of L's favorite novels was *Gilead*. In that book, filled
with heartbreak, Marilynne Robinson writes:

*In every important way we are such secrets from one
another, and I do believe that there is a separate language in each of us, also a separate aesthetics and a
separate jurisprudence. . . . We take fortuitous resem-
blances among us to be actual likeness. . . . But all
that really just allows us to coexist with the inviola-
ble, intraversable, and utterly vast spaces between us.*

What Scott had done had exposed the spaces between
us. And I don't mean between *us*—him and me—but between all of us, all the time. Love collapses these spaces,
but not absolutely. When I sent books, I hoped that some of
what these writers said might form a bridge—washed-out
though I knew it would be, when the tide rose again.

IN OCTOBER, I ATTENDED THE LAW SCHOOL'S PUBLIC
interest awards dinner. Bryan Stevenson, the executive director of the Equal Justice Initiative in Alabama, was the
keynote speaker and recipient of the National Public Service Award. I didn't know anything about Stevenson. This
was 2010, before his TED Talk, book, and movie. When
he got up to address the room, there was the usual hum of
side conversations and caterers pouring water and asking,
Red or white?, but moments in, the noise dropped away. My
memories from that night are crisp. I remember the black
dress I was wearing; the stiff white tablecloth over the round
table; the small white dish on which a black-clothed server

had placed a roll from a basket with tongs; the faces of the professors, staff, and students in the banquet hall, rapt and blinking, turned in unison toward the stage and the sound of truth, as if drawn to a very bright light. Stevenson was describing a young man he represented in court, and the absurdity of a system that decides almost magically, as if by waving a wand, to try juvenile offenders as adults, despite their scientifically proven deficiencies in brain development. His response: to write a motion to the court titled "Motion to try my poor, 14-year-old, Black, male client like a privileged, White, 75-year-old corporate executive."

I thought of how, in Scott's case, he was being tried as an adult in criminal court, which made him eligible for the most serious sentences. But in a civil suit proceeding concurrently, the law deemed him a minor, thereby triggering his parents' legal liability for his actions. An adult in criminal court and a child in civil. The worst kind of magic.

Then Stevenson spoke about darkness. He said that sometimes what was required of us is a willingness to pay attention to darkness, a willingness to be in hopeless places as a witness. I felt a door open. To the extent I had been attuned to darkness lately, but also as a child, this was the first time I'd heard it described not only as a liability but also as a strength.

Two years later, I would meet Bryan Stevenson and tell him that he changed my life. And after that, he would help me understand the legal landscape of Scott's case. But that night, all I knew was that he had given me something I was looking for. He made me feel that I could be useful, make something, make sense of what felt senseless. He radiated moral clarity, which is exactly what I'd been missing.

When Stevenson writes that *mercy belongs to the undeserving*, he's dropping us into the dark space between justice and fairness. We act as if *fairness* and *justice* are synonyms, but they are not. Fairness is technical, a word tied to the world we can see: numbers and volumes and scales. But justice holds what is seen and unseen. Justice lifts us up, delivers us into our hearts. Mercy may be unfair in some technical sense, but it is just, because mercy has the muscle to transmute. Stevenson writes:

> *It's when mercy is least expected that it's most potent—strong enough to break the cycle of victimization and victimhood, retribution and suffering. It has the power to heal the psychic harm and injuries that lead to aggression and violence, abuse of power, mass incarceration.*

Stevenson isn't a theorist. What he knows about mercy he has learned by paying attention to darkness.

PART II

HOW WOULD
YOU WRITE IT

Now, he told me, I could see what
humanity was worth. It could form
the conception of justice, but could
not trust its flesh to provide judges....
There was ruin everywhere.

—REBECCA WEST,
The Fountain Overflows

I remember people disappearing.

My grandmother and her big bosom layered in gold jewelry and Jungle Gardenia left our lives for good after a fight with my father, her son-in-law. The fight was about a telephone call she'd made to me, while my parents were out of the country. My father was writing a novel set in London, and my mother had gone to England with him for a week. My brother and I were home with my mother's friend Linda. I was about eight. On the phone, my grandmother asked me why my mother wouldn't let me see her more often. And other questions, too—like, *What's she so mad at me about? Why is she trying to hurt me?*—and I remember not having an answer for any of them, and feeling as if my mother, or I, was in trouble or about to be. My grandmother's voice sounded strange, like she was talking underwater, as if her words themselves were melting. Linda took the phone away when I started to cry. A year or so before, my mother had left me with my grandmother at the Ritz, where she always stayed when she visited us in Boston. A few hours later, my mother came back to find my grandmother asleep on the hotel room bed while I sat on the floor watching TV. I didn't understand why my mother was so un-nerved by it then. I didn't know she was remembering her own childhood, the bottle of wine in her mother's lingerie drawer, the bottle of pills on the nightstand. I've tried to be in touch with my grandmother again, but we've not spoken since the night she called me while my parents were in London.

This wasn't the first or last time my father had a fight with someone and the relationship ended, but most of the other departures from our lives were not his fault. My beautiful godmother, the writer Alice Adams—I remember her always with a silk scarf tied around her neck—died of a heart attack in her sleep. Cancer took my mother's best friend, Garnette, who made me laugh so hard I almost peed my pants, who made me feel chosen. My friend Thomas, who was doing algebra while we were all still counting on our fingers, was pulled from his father's arms by a riptide while swimming in the Atlantic.

When my parents sat me down to tell me about Thomas, it was the end of summer and the garden was hanging over itself in the heat, the foxgloves waist-high, the lilies dropping their yellow skirts down to the dirt like tired dancers. Fifth grade was about to start. I'd asked, with tears in my eyes, as we sat around the table on the back porch, if they were going to tell me I couldn't wear my new leather jacket on the first day of school. My godfather, Tellis, had given me the jacket—Tellis was a Vietnam vet who rode motorcycles, and the jacket matched his own. *No, honey*, my mother said. *It's about Thomas.* My mother's voice wobbled slightly. She cleared her throat. She told me what happened. When I opened my mouth to speak, all that came out was a very long *why?* And then I cried on my mother's shoulder, thinking how stupid I had been about the jacket and how the word *riptide* sounded as terrible as what it had done.

In this little house in Massachusetts, a white saltbox with periwinkle shutters, my parents tried to build a life for me and my brother, Sam, far away from the pain of their own childhoods. A pain they made no bones about, even when we were young. I knew my parents were survivors. They never tried to hide their contempt for the stories they'd climbed out of.

My father grew up on a chicken farm in Alabama. In the mornings, before school, it was his job to collect eggs, and the pecking chickens drew blood from his hands. He still hates chickens. His father, my grandfather, whom we called Pop, used to beat my grandmother Evelyne, and my father, who was the youngest of four children, used to jump on Pop's back to try to get him to stop.

Evelyne married Pop, whose Christian name was Herschel, when she was fourteen years old. She had her first child, my uncle Freddy (who died in his forties after open-heart surgery), when she was fifteen. Her age reflects the times but also an eagerness to escape the ferocity and responsibility of her original home. Her mother, Mama Leonard, was a textbook hypochondriac who took to bed for weeks, leaving Evelyne in charge of the household and her younger brothers and sisters. And when Mama Leonard wasn't laid up, she was vicious. One day she shattered an electrical meter's bulbous glass cover with my great-aunt Joyce's skull. It's no wonder Evelyne wanted to escape. That she escaped into a situation no better than the one she was born into is not surprising—people have an uncanny ability in this regard. And for Herschel's part, the only thing I know about his father, Daddy Perry, is that he used to grope little children and everyone knew it and nobody said anything about it because they were afraid of him.

My mother grew up only a few states west, in Texas, but a world away in terms of scenery—a world of country club swimming pools, debutante gowns, and upholstered boudoir chairs in Neiman Marcus fitting rooms. But money didn't save her from the broad brushstrokes of my father's life: cruelty, abuse, and secrets. Cruelty ran through my mother's father like the scotch in his blood. He used to beat her brothers, my uncles, and force them to eat food off the toilet. He loved women—the younger the better. His fifth wife was roughly the same age as my mother, his oldest daughter. When I think of my mother's childhood, I think of her poems, and one in particular, called "One Day":

Clean sheets, a silk couch like a gold mine
a tall screen, blue mountains on ebony where a small man
walked into the mountains, walked away.

Do not run your hands over these things.

One day my mother set up tables
on the marble floor of the foyer. Men
straightened and locked the legs. Women
laid them with linen and china, patterns
of brilliant birds and plants,

then one collapsed, its stark legs buckling.

Bright shards of wings and leaves, orange and purple
littered the marble. So beautiful
said my half brother, leaning over the banister,
the most beautiful fucking thing.

The brother in "One Day" is Roy. He and my mother grew up together, protecting each other from fighting grown-ups, banding together against chaos. But he was murdered when he was nineteen, shot by a teenager's stolen gun. I don't know whether it's Roy who fills the poem with heartbreak, or if it's the buckling legs, the shards of wing, or the small man walking away into the mountains, which is what my mother wanted to do and what she eventually did, what Roy would never do.

When my parents left the South, they were escaping the violence of their own homes but also a bigger, cultural violence, a racism and bigotry, a burning torch for the Confederacy. So there was no romanticizing the South in our home. *Southern hospitality* was a joke to them—*hospitable to whom?* But underneath the derision was a certain kind of pain, the strain of growing up as outsiders in a culture that felt foreign even though it was home. This, I think, is partly what they found in each other, and what they recognized when they met at a creative writing program in Vermont in their twenties: the feeling of not belonging, a sheen of survival.

They never stopped acting like survivors. Even after they'd settled down, they retained a posture of looking over their shoulders. They looked back, and they remembered even as they said they wanted to forget. And perhaps because they were writers, much of this looking back took rhetorical form: they told us hundreds of stories about the past, some of which were sad and some of which were funny. All of which made history real.

The time my mother and Roy found an old cardboard box and went down the back staircase in it—a game they called *going over Niagara Falls in a barrel*—until Roy smashed into the wall at the bottom of the stairs so hard he broke off his toe—*hanging by a thread*—and tracked blood through the house trying to get help. The time Roy put a dummy bloodied with ketchup into the middle of a busy road and almost caused an accident. The way Pop used to say, if someone asked him to pass the potatoes, *Eat somethin' close to ya.*

I was full of these stories and voices by the time I was ten, which had a kind of bifurcating effect: we were here, and we were there. Or *they* were here—the ghosts and the places of the past crowding up the present. On a recent trip to visit my parents, who are now in their late sixties, we were sitting around in the kitchen and my mother came up behind my father while he was peeling potatoes and hugged him, her heart against his back, her arms wrapped around his middle, and said, apropos of nothing but a train of thought she was following in her own mind, *Well, you just have to think how fucking far we've come.*

After they graduated from the MFA program and got married, they lived for a few years in San Francisco, where I was born, and then moved to Massachusetts, to the white house with the big backyard across from the woods and sloping hills of a golf course, where we went sledding in the winter. Sam arrived the first year we were there, a couple of days before Thanksgiving, in a snowstorm. Our new neighbors shoveled the drive and brought a whole Thanksgiving dinner, including pie. In the spring, my parents dug a garden in front for flowers and planted cucumbers and tomatoes in the back. The forsythia bush lit up like stars outside our windows, and I woke up early to the crows gossiping in the old maple trees. After church on Sundays we went to McDonald's and I'd always get the same thing: a hamburger

Happy Meal, but I'd eat it without the bun. I liked to save the bun for the seagulls that swarmed the parking lot for scraps. Sometimes my father and I would go to McDonald's on Saturdays, too, or after school, and sit in the car throwing French fries out the window for the gulls. It was fun to make a frenzy.

My parents were trying to start over, to do it differently. And though we grew up eating grits and listening to country music and my friends said my parents talked funny, these were the exceptions that proved the rule. In the Northeast, my parents loved us with fierceness, like they were trying to save us from something. Like they were trying to save themselves.

But inheritance is a force that overwhelms intention. By definition it overtakes geography and time. Despite their efforts, heartbreak was passed down to us through molecules and memory. It showed up in my mother's fear and my father's rage and my mother's fear of my father's rage. It showed up in his bottle of scotch, which was tucked away inside the dining room cabinet and glowed like something nuclear through the cabinet's pane-glass door. It showed up in the stream of stories from a time before. It showed up in our hands: once a fortune-teller at a party took my right palm and traced the life line with her index finger. *So much heartbreak*, she said, pointing to the tiny interruptions and cross marks as evidence. *I'm an alcoholic*, I told her. *And so are my parents. Well, that explains it*, she said.

But these crosses come from more than drinking. It's a national inheritance; it's generational and general. Half of my family history I share with Scott, and like so many families in America, the half we share has perpetuated and endured an ordinary, routine violence. I always think of this paragraph from *Housekeeping*, one of the best descriptions I've ever read of a certain piece of America:

> *What with the lake and the railroads, and what with the blizzards and floods and barn fires and forest fires and the general availability of shotguns and bear traps and homemade liquor and dynamite, what with the prevalence of loneliness and religion and the rages and ecstasies they induce, and the closeness of families, violence was inevitable.*

Husbands beating their wives; husbands and wives beating their children. Even the most conservative view of epigenetics acknowledges that the effects of violence are passed on.*

Meanwhile, we only barely admit that our national story starts with bloodshed. I've come to believe that all this

---

* In one study, the offspring of mice who were tortured while smelling the scent of cherries don't experience *fear* of the smell of cherries, as their parents did, but all exhibited a heightened sensitivity to cherries. These mice were raised by nonbiological parents, to rule out the role of nurture. The trend carried over to the third generation, too.

private, domestic violence is inseparable from the violence at our foundations, carried out in the name of progress and economy. The killing of indigenous people, the stripping of any possible natural resource, slavery, lynching, Jim Crow. Historically, if not genetically, we are all the inheritors of heartbreak and violence. We can't recover from this history, says Bryan Stevenson, until we deal with it. Dealing with it starts in telling the truth. I believe the same is true of families.

My father spends half the year back in Mobile now, his hometown in Alabama. It is a great surprise to him that he has *chosen* to return to the South—but going back felt like going home, which felt right. He and my mother spend the winter in a little house a few streets over from Michael Donald Avenue. Michael Donald Avenue used to be Herndon Avenue, but it was renamed in 2006 to remember Michael Donald, who was lynched in 1981, hung from a tree on Herndon Avenue. This is one of the most recent officially recognized lynchings in American history. Donald's mother, Beulah Mae (Greggory) Donald, brought a civil suit for wrongful death against the United Klans of America (UKA), the group the attackers belonged to. In 1987, a jury awarded her $7 million in damages, which bankrupted the UKA. The case set a new precedent for civil legal action for damages against racist hate groups, which is still a chief strategy for the Southern Poverty Law Center and other civil rights groups. Meanwhile, the criminal trial convicted both murderers and two accomplices. In 1997, one (Henry Hays) was executed and the other (James "Tiger" Knowles) was sentenced to life in prison. Knowles was seventeen at the time of the murder. Hays's execution was the first time Alabama sentenced a white man to die for killing a Black man since 1913.

The point is, our violent history is not so historical, in the sense that it's not far away from us. And though I'm not saying a legacy of violence is *why* Scott murdered Ryan—nothing so simple or straightforward as that—I have to admit that when I think about the chicken farm in Alabama, the dirt and the blood and the private and political cruelty we come from, it makes me wonder about chickens coming home to roost. Scott's violence felt extreme and shocking, like an aberration, but in tracing back the thread, I could also describe it as a culmination. Not a departure, but a return. And I could trace a similar thread backward from almost any of the white boys who are making headlines by turning their pain into a weapon, many of whom descend from people who watched lynchings for sport, who sent lynching postcards in the mail, and not very long ago. In *Without Sanctuary: Lynching Photography in America*, Hilton Als writes: *I didn't like looking at these pictures, but once I looked, the events documented in them occurred in my mind over and over again. . . . And it is as one that I felt my neck snap and my heart break, while looking at these pictures.*

———

THE FIRST LETTER SCOTT WROTE TO ME WAS A THANK-
you note. It was a few weeks after the awards dinner with
Bryan Stevenson. I held the small envelope, which was slightly
grayed, and stared at his name in pencil in the upper-left
corner. I felt a quick drop in my stomach. I opened it as if
it might contain something I was waiting for. Inside was
a piece of lined notebook paper and a brief, polite note,
thanking me for the books, signed *Love, Scott*, in childlike
cursive. I had not been waiting for this.

I read the note and then folded it back into the envelope and tucked it between the pages of a book and put
the book back on the shelf. The word *love* caught me off
guard. I knew it might be a nicety rather than a heart-
felt expression, but still I balked—did I love this boy in
jail who'd done this unspeakable thing? I didn't know. I
didn't know him well enough to love him, and part of me
wanted to push it away, to reject the bond it suggested.
But he was Louise's first grandson, and my father's great-
nephew, and there is something that made my heart reach
out to him, in spite of itself. I was too scant in my own
personhood then to think through these questions mean-
ingfully. So I buried the letter in my bookcase, and I didn't
write him back. I didn't write him back for years. He kept
sending notes, and I kept sending books, but I didn't write
him back.

THAT FALL OF 2L I'D SIGNED UP FOR JUVENILE JUS-
tice, and when Scott's letter came, I was knee-deep in the
history of the system.

Before 1899, the law made no meaningful distinction between offenders based on age. Children and teenagers were
tried in the same courtrooms and sentenced to the same
jails as grown-ups. But following a concerted movement by
a group of advocates, mostly progressive, barrier-breaking
women like Julia Lathrop and Lucy Flower, the first juvenile
court was established in Cook County, Illinois, authorized
by the Illinois Juvenile Court Act of 1899. The act gave the
state jurisdiction over neglected or delinquent children under the age of sixteen, which emanates from the ancient doctrine of *parens patriae*, or the state as parent. The juvenile
court's influence spread until it became a network of courtrooms across the country, eventually known as the juvenile
justice system. By 1925, there was a juvenile court in every
state except for Maine and Wyoming.

What set these courtrooms apart was the purported purpose to rehabilitate instead of punish. This is what advocates had been pushing for. The argument ran this way: to
treat young people as having the same moral culpability as
adults was wrongheaded, and to ignore their potential to
change—a key feature of youth and impressionability—was
cruel.

The courtrooms were also less formal, and this took a few forms: first, records of the court were to be confidential in order to minimize stigma—a practice mostly preserved today; second, the act provided for relaxed procedures within the court, in order to make things less frightening and to allow a judge to handle each case with a tailor-made focus; third, children were not to be locked up with grownups, and children under seven were not to be locked up at all. This, of course, required the creation of juvenile jails and reform schools.

Predictably, the wide discretion afforded to judges became more problematic than helpful. Two young people, coming before the court for the same crime, were likely to get different responses from whomever the judge happened to be that day, depending mostly on what his mood was, and what he felt, personally, about that child's look, race, demeanor, and perceived capacity to change. It's also worth noting that in 1903, four years after this act was passed, there were already exceptions: certain juveniles were transferred to adult courtrooms and tried as adults, which was a decision made by the prosecutor.

It took more than sixty years for these concerns to make their way to the Supreme Court. When they did, the Court voted to reformalize proceedings for young people, based on the idea that formality was the only way to produce consistent, nonprejudicial results and to provide young people with the due-process rights promised to all citizens, regardless of age.*

The history of the system took up the first couple of weeks of my Juvenile Justice class. Then we moved on to a series of guest lecturers from actors inside the modern system: a probation officer, the superintendent of a detention facility, a local sheriff.

Outside of class, I signed up to teach at Hillcrest Juvenile Hall, a detention center about thirty minutes north along the peninsula, in San Mateo. Once a week, I would drive with three other law students up Highway 280, one of the most scenic stretches of paved road in the country. Inside the facility's brick administration building, we presented our IDs and were escorted by a guard through a series of gates and doors. The classroom was an open space rung around with heavy doored cells, each with its own tiny window, like portholes on a ship. For an hour at a time, we taught lessons on government and law, focusing on individual rights. When can you refuse to hand over your backpack to a police officer? What are your Miranda rights?

---

* *In re Gault*, 387 U.S. 1 (1967) (holding that children have many of the same legal rights as adults in criminal court, including the right to an attorney, the right to remain silent, the right to notice of the charges, and the right to a full hearing on the merits of the case); *Kent v. United States*, 383 U.S. 541 (1966) (a juvenile court does not have unlimited *parens patriae* power); *In re Winship*, 397 U.S. 358 (1970) (holding that for adjudications of delinquency, the standard of proof required is the same as for criminal cases: beyond a reasonable doubt).

The students were different from Scott in almost every way except for age. They were not locked up for murder—their crimes were truancy and delinquency, sometimes gang-related violence. Most were not white; most hadn't grown up in nice houses in the suburbs, with schedules full of AP classes and soccer practices. These facts made their stories easier to understand. The system was rigged against them from the get-go. Their stories included the *mitigating evidence* that allowed for an untroubled morality and therefore unchecked empathy—what I couldn't feel for Scott.

Which is to say, if I was walking into those armored classrooms and sitting next to these students in response to where Scott was, the connection was oblique. And yet I remember the pull of a thread, a thread that stretched back to a small cell in Louisiana. That was the feeling I often had that fall as I hustled around the periphery of these stories and settings, these concepts on a syllabus that were, for Scott and the students at Hillcrest, the facts of their lives. I was unable to face Scott and the questions he raised, because I was afraid. Instead, I responded indirectly, doing what I felt I could, adjacent to what I couldn't.

My professor for Juvenile Justice was Joan Petersilia, who died in 2019 of ovarian cancer. At the end of the semester, she wrote me this email:

> *I am so grateful to have had you in my class. I really enjoyed getting to know you, and I do hope that it*

*may have given you "power" in thinking about your
cousin and his situation. My heart really continually
goes out to you and his family.*

Professor Petersilia was uncommon at the law school. She
was warm and approachable, engaging in normal small talk,
socially fluent. She was a practitioner committed to policy
change rather than to scholarship above all else. I don't remember talking with her about Scott, though I obviously
did, but I do remember hoping that the class, and everything
else I was doing that fall, might make something right, might
give me a way to hold what I hadn't been able to hold.

IN KATE CHOPIN'S "THE STORY OF AN HOUR," MRS.
Mallard's friends are afraid, because of her weak heart, to
tell her that her husband is dead. They try to break the news
gently, to avoid inducing sudden heart failure. When they
do finally tell her, she is not heartbroken, but overcome
with joy at the idea of freedom from her unhappy marriage.
But when she finds out that the rumors of her husband's
death were false, her heart *does* stop and she does die. The
doctors say she died *of heart disease—of joy that kills.* Of
course they were wrong about the joy, but the point is—at
least narratively—it was reasonable that either grief or joy
might send her into cardiac arrest.

These days, there are several meanings camped out under
the single word *heartbreak*. In common usage, a toddler's

misunderstanding is *heartbreaking*, with the tented eye-brows of tenderness; the beef brisket sandwich is *heart-breakingly good*, with an eye roll of ecstasy; the rusted light of sunset can *break your heart*. This breadth of meaning is confusing. But if not too long ago we believed either sorrow or joy could stop the heart, it makes more sense. According to Victorian doctors, all it took was intense emotion, either pleasure or pain. In other words, it's heartbreaking because it pierces your heart and the heart can be pierced by loss but also love or beauty, fleeting innocence, a sandwich, or a sunset.

Still, when a word expands to hold too much, it loses meaning. And in its range of modern uses, the word *heart-break* has been sillied. We've disarmed it by using it ironi-cally, or sappily, in overstatements. Because our experience is informed by the language we have to describe that experi-ence, the loss of *heartbreak* as a serious word indicates our lost ability to *feel* our hearts, to recognize a pain there and the seriousness of that pain.

But the wisdom stays in the body. Recently, on the radio, I heard the civil rights activist Ruby Sales talk about how she learned to ask a radical question of people: *Where does it hurt?* Without thinking, I lift my hand and place it just above my heart.

THE FIRST TIME I SAW REAL POWER IN THE LAW WAS when I started reading the big constitutional cases, the class-action lawsuits that changed history. The force was blunt and mighty. Smashing things appealed to me. So for the second half of my second year of law school, I left California to head back to D.C., where I could be with L and earn course credits working at the ACLU's National Prison Project.

NPP was a small and rugged group, headed by a soft-spoken, kind, and whip-smart attorney named David. Our job was to bring class-action lawsuits against prisons that were violating people's constitutional rights. Not letting them read their Bibles and Korans, for instance (First Amendment), or routinely engaging in cruel and unusual punishment (Eighth Amendment). Every lawyer there was shrewd and dedicated, trending toward a refreshing and stoic nerdiness, glasses and plaid button-down shirts. Mostly my day-to-day work involved editing motions and court communications. But for a series of weeks toward the end of my stint, I was brought onto two cases, which had been won several years earlier, in which a judge had ordered a consent decree. A consent decree is a legally binding agreement between two parties that acts as a kind of settlement. For instance, a consent decree might require the Mississippi Department of Corrections to protect juveniles in custody from sexual assault.

The problem is enforcement. I don't remember whose job it was, in this case, to monitor the consent decree—to make sure that the prison was complying—but it became clear quickly that if we didn't, no one would. This is an obvious but demoralizing reality of judicial power. A judge declares what *should* happen, not what *will* happen.

The mechanism we had for monitoring the consent decree was communicating with former clients still in prison. And so my job became to read their letters. Hundreds of letters, written by hand, in pencil. My supervising attorney told me to skim the letters for abuses to catalog on a spreadsheet, but I have never been good at skimming. Instead, I shut the door to my office and disappeared into the paragraphs. I heard each man's voice; I saw his hand moving across the paper. Sometimes I looked him up based on his inmate number, to learn what he was in for. Rape, murder, burglary. I became so immersed in these letters that when someone knocked on the door or the phone rang, I startled. It was disorienting to be back inside reality—my reality, well-lit, clean, safe.

The reality of the letters featured sweltering cells rife with rats, mice, and fire ants; broken bones from run-ins with guards too quick to use force; pepper spray, a host of racial epithets, and vulgar sexual innuendo, especially against inmates with extreme mental illness; medications forgotten or overprescribed; reading materials withheld; broken plumbing (*ping-pong toilets*, as the inmates called them—meaning what went down in one cell would come up in another) and floods. One man at Angola woke up with a snake in his cell.

One morning a pile of letters arrived on my desk, all

written on the same day. Something had happened. Each letter told pieces of the same story.

Someone in a cell was screaming for help. He was saying, "Help me, I can't breathe," and crying out in pain. (I would remember this man's cries, *I can't breathe*, three years later, when the words became a refrain after Eric Garner was killed by police officers in 2014, and then again, in 2020, when George Floyd was killed by police officers. *I can't breathe* on signs and T-shirts at protests, an anthem of the Black Lives Matter movement.) The men on the block started banging metal cups on their heavy cell doors, trying to get the guards' attention. But the guards never came. At which point the men sat down to write to us. They didn't know if the screaming man was still alive. *Please look into this*, they wrote. *Please, can you help?*

I brought the incident to my supervising attorney. He pulled up a database of prisoners, and sure enough, on the day after the date of the letters, one man, identified by his DOC number, was marked DECEASED.

I didn't know then that the letters I was reading previewed the letters I would read from Scott years later, after he was transferred to Angola.

Please, can you help?

READING LETTERS FROM MEN IN PRISON REMINDED me of the intimacy of letters. Holding an object that the writer held—tracing the lines of another's hand—collapses the space and time between writing and reading. Perhaps this intimacy is what explains the market for murderers' letters, some thrill attached to holding what was made by hands that killed. Murderers like the Australians Ivan Milat, who killed seven people, and Daniel Holdom, who murdered Karlie Pearce-Stevenson and her two-year-old daughter, Khandalyce Pearce, keep themselves in the news by writing letters from prison. Milat's letters to his nephew were published in 2016. Holdom's letters were turned into a podcast by the *Daily Telegraph*.

Recently I discovered one of Scott's letters for sale on a site called *Death Merchant*. A picture of the letter appears next to his mugshot, along with a description of the murder and of Scott himself: a *normal* teenager who *randomly killed his victim, a stranger to him.* The synopsis describes how Ryan was on a bike ride and had become separated from his family; how Scott *repeatedly stabbed* him and then *killed him by slitting his throat.* It describes Ryan fighting back, his *defensive wounds.* It describes Scott as *exceptionally bright with a 4.0 GPA.* And how he had come to identify with a serial killer from a Showtime drama, which helped him *establish a powerful sense of an evil identity*:

> *Due to his age he wasn't eligible for the Death Penalty, instead he received life in prison without the possibility of parole.*
>
> *This is a 2 page handwritten letter (the first page*

is front and back, the second just front) and it is writ-
ten on miniature lined paper. It comes with an enve-
lope filled out in his hand as well.

Available for purchase below.

Death Merchant's website, which describes itself as a re-
tail company of *true crime & murderabilia*, isn't live anymore, but their profile picture on Facebook is a skeleton hand
holding a human heart, severed arteries and veins sprawling
outward and upward like crimson branches.

UNABLE TO COLLAPSE THE BOUNDARIES BETWEEN US
by sending my own letter, I kept sending Scott books. He'd
started asking for titles through his father, who would email
me and a few other family and friends around the holidays
and Scott's birthday with a list of requests. Sometimes I'd
send my own selections. That Christmas I sent him *The
Complete Works of Shakespeare*, which he finished in its
entirety by the spring.

Next I sent the Lord of the Rings series; Philip Pullman's
His Dark Materials trilogy; biographies of Thomas Jeffer-
son, Abraham Lincoln, John Lennon, and Paul Farmer; *The
Complete Sherlock Holmes*, volumes I and II; the Master
and Commander series; and then a handful of novels, including old and new titles like *Cold Mountain* and *The Once
and Future King*. Scott liked *The Amazing Adventures of
Kavalier & Clay* so much that he decided to keep it, rather

than passing it on to the jail's library, which would free up space in his cell for a new book. He was allowed only five at a time, including his Bible. In *Kavalier & Clay*, Michael Chabon writes:

> *We have the idea that our hearts, once broken, scar over with an indestructible tissue that prevents their ever breaking again in quite the same place; but as Sammy watched Joe, he felt the heartbreak of that day in 1935 when the Mighty Molecule had gone away for good.*

When it comes to inheritance, the idea of scars as fault lines rather than reinforcement bears out.

THE MOST COMMON CONTEXTS FOR THE WORD *HEARTBREAK* in the news are, in no important order:

1. Sports
2. Addiction
3. Disaster
4. Children
5. Celebrity romance

The last is what we'd expect. The first four disclose heartbreak's essence, across and beyond the particular details.

In sportscasting, which is, in fact, the leader in terms

of frequency, lost games are constantly reported as "heart-breaking." The importance of the game or team doesn't seem to matter much. When the loss is an upset, the heart-break graduates to "devastating" or "unimaginable."

My father screams at the radio when the Red Sox season goes south, which—for all their modern winning—it still does more often than not. When Chapel Hill loses to Duke, you want to give my uncle a wide berth. The hurt is palpable, but the loss is hardly real. When your team loses a game, you're losing victory, something you never had and didn't do anything to secure yourself and something you weren't guaranteed. All that's been lost is an imagined future, a chance. Even in the audience, there's something unbearable to the human heart about losing a chance.

Losing a chance at victory leaves fans weeping in the stands. Losing a chance for freedom leaves families weeping in a courtroom. In some ways, this is the sting every death leaves us with, too—not only the loss of present love and presence, but the life you imagined with that love still here, punctuating the future with milestones. When your child dies (or goes to prison for life), you lose him, and also the chance to watch him grow up, graduate, fall in love. The chance to call someone back, tell the truth, say thank you. Death obviates chance.

In sports, I think it's practice that we're after, a place to feel the full spectrum from victory to loss, heartbreak to windfall joy, when the stakes are low. Fans get to play out

love and hope and then survive that hope being dashed—
"devastating heartbreak," "an unimaginable blow"—
knowing that, unlike with other life losses, there'll be another game, another season.

IN THE FALL OF MY LAST YEAR OF LAW SCHOOL, I
signed up for Ethics, Evidence, Clinic, and a new class called
Veterans Courts. I was excited to tell my godfather, Tellis,
about my veterans class. Tellis had received a Purple Heart
for his service in Vietnam. He was kind and silly, but he still
wore Marine Corps T-shirts with slogans like *Shoot 'em
all and let God sort it out*. I never pressed him on whether
he really endorsed the slogans. I have a feeling he did, since
that's the choice that war presents: kill or be killed.

Tellis didn't survive only war. He was a survivor times
a hundred. I had some sense of this when I was little, but
I didn't know the details until I was older. For instance, I
was amazed by his *two belly buttons*, which he'd make a
big show about when we were little, lifting up his T-shirt
and letting us marvel, but when I grew up, I learned that
one hole was from a bullet he'd put in his own body, one of
several suicide attempts he survived. He survived growing
up as a Black teenager in segregated Boston. He survived a
few different stints in jail.

Tellis would often stay with me and Sam when my parents went out or traveled, and he always let me stay up late

watching *Cops*, *America's Most Wanted*, and *The X-Files*. I still know the theme songs for these shows by heart, and when I hear them, I still think of him.

Tellis called me right when classes were getting started that fall. A week later, I still hadn't called him back. I hadn't even listened to his message when my mother called to tell me he had died. Sixty-two years old, dropped dead of a heart attack. I hit the floor in the middle of my one-room cottage in Los Altos. I felt everything draining away. Then the tears came—Tellis was a second father to me. And then regret—I hadn't called him back. I would never get a chance to make that right.

A TRIAL DATE WAS SET FOR SCOTT. I LEARNED HE AND his lawyers were planning to plead not guilty by reason of insanity (NGRI). For the winter quarter, I signed up for Mental Health Law.

The first thing I learned about NGRI is that it's little used and not often successful. It presents a difficult legal standard to meet. And it also suffers a PR problem stemming from those first two words—*not guilty*—a bad framing, because of course everyone who pleads NGRI *is* guilty in a factual sense. A difficult hurdle to surmount in the realm of public opinion.

This PR problem was made famous in 1981, when John Hinckley Jr. shot President Ronald Reagan, as well as Secret Service agent Timothy McCarthy, District of Columbia police officer Tom Delahanty, and Reagan's press secretary James Brady. Hinkley was tried and found not guilty by reason of insanity, and the verdict caused public outrage. An ABC News poll conducted the day after the verdict found that three-quarters of Americans felt "justice had not been done." People decried what they saw as a loophole that let a murderer walk free.

Hinckley's reason for trying to kill the president was that he was trying to impress Jodie Foster. He'd become obsessed with Foster and the movie *Taxi Driver*, in which Robert De Niro's character can't sleep and loses touch with reality and starts plotting to assassinate a presidential candidate. Foster also appears in the film, as a twelve-year-old prostitute named Iris. In a letter to *The New York Times*, Hinckley described his act as *the greatest love offering in the history of the world. . . . I am Napoleon and she is Josephine. I am Romeo and she is Juliet.* Which is to say, he was insane. His defense's medical expert diagnosed Hinckley with schizophrenia. Even the prosecution's appointed doctor agreed that Hinckley suffered from narcissistic and schizoid personality disorders, plus depression and passive-aggressive behavior (though somehow still deemed him legally sane). The judge ruled in favor of the defense. Hinckley was transferred to a psych ward.

Was this justice? In response to the verdict, several states changed their laws. Utah, Montana, and Idaho abolished the insanity defense entirely. Delaware put forward a new plea: Guilty but Mentally Ill.* And Congress passed the Insanity Defense Reform Act of 1984, a legislative effort meant to raise the bar for proving insanity. Today, different states use different tests for establishing legal insanity, but the vast majority rely on the guidelines laid out by Congress in the eighties, which have their roots in an early standard called the M'Naghten test.† Scott's crime was tried in such a state, which meant, practically speaking, his attorney would have to prove that Scott didn't know killing Ryan was wrong.

It's interesting how upset we can get about something so unlikely and infrequent. Before *Hinkley*, the insanity defense was used in only 2 percent of cases and was successful

---

* *Guilty but Mentally Ill* allows a defendant to be convicted of a crime but sentenced to a mental institution instead of a prison. The sentence feels more accurate, though whether it's "better" is unclear, given the state of many mental institutions, which are, in terms of their conditions, no better than the average prison.

† The M'Naghten test, which comes from a British common-law case, defines insanity as the defendant's *inability to appreciate the wrongfulness of his act*. The inquiry investigates knowledge. What did the defendant know? In the original case, decided in 1843, Daniel M'Naghten, a woodcutter from Glasgow, killed Edward Drummond, the secretary of the British prime minister. M'Naghten said he believed the secretary was conspiring against him. During his trial, Lord Chief Justice Tindal told the jury that the central question was whether, *at the time the act in question was committed, the prisoner had or had not the use of his understanding, so as to know that he was doing a wrong or wicked act.*

Congress's act also made the test more stringent by shifting two procedural markers: first, they shifted the burden of proof to the defense, and second, they made the standard of evidence to carry this burden *clear and convincing evidence*, which is one step up from *a preponderance of evidence*.

less than 30 percent of the time. Today it's used in about 1 percent of cases and similarly unsuccessful. But our anxieties, rages, and fears are rarely proportional to likelihood. If our fears were rational, we'd be more afraid of terminal sunstroke than airplane crashes. More afraid of driving than being raped and murdered. This does not reflect my experience of fear.

My professor in Mental Health Law had gray hair and wore glasses and was smart in a way that made his thinking sometimes rambling, but he also had noticeable arm muscles, which you could see because he wore T-shirts and jeans to class, and when he arrived, you had the feeling he might have come in straight from surfing or tinkering with some new project in his garage. He paired all this with a welcome unpretentiousness. He didn't care about decorum, the way many professors did; there was no theater or cold calling. Just history, ideas, stories, and questions. And though we learned the law, he seemed to be most interested in the philosophy underlying that law.

What *are* the philosophical underpinnings for the insanity defense? Some say the justification is free will: we can hold people criminally responsible for their actions because we believe they freely choose those actions. But people who are mentally ill are not free. They act under duress. And therefore, they cannot be legally culpable. Other legal scholars argue against this justification as simplistic and misguiding. The insanity defense, they say, is not about free will, but rationality. Legal insanity requires a finding not of captivity but *irrationality*.

Our class was in the late afternoon, twice a week, and when we got out, all the light had drained from the sky. I walked through campus in the dark, thinking about insanity. Our professor let me write my final paper on the rarely invoked deific decree doctrine, in which someone pleads not guilty because their crime was inspired by the voice of God.

I did not call my parents or Aunt Louise to tell them how unlikely a successful insanity defense would be for Scott. Aunt Louise had never sounded hopeful anyway. Though I always thought her hopelessness was a symptom of grief, after studying the subject in school, I understood it was a purely rational posture. Proof of, if anything, sanity.

INSIDE AND OUTSIDE OF THE COURTROOM, DEFENSES fail us. Often they're expensive. C. S. Lewis—who wrote a slim treatise on grief after his wife died of cancer at the age of forty-five—wrote, of the heart:

> *If you want to make sure of keeping it intact, you must give it to no one, not even an animal. Wrap it carefully round with hobbies and little luxuries; avoid all entanglements.*

But so much is lost in the effort to save ourselves and our hearts. This is what I mean by expensive.

Take, for instance, the addict who tries and tries and tries to save himself from any primary experience of the world—at the cost of what? Eventually his life. In the news, addiction earns the adjective *heartbreaking* almost as frequently as sports. Sometimes these headlines point to the wreckage: *Son's addiction ends in mother's heartbreak*. Sometimes its rampant ubiquity: *Juno's heroin heartbreak*. And when a famous musician or actor overdoses, the word connotes the ongoing theme of something irretrievably lost—the impossibility of further contribution, a silence. When Philip Seymour Hoffman died from a heroin overdose after decades of being clean, a sober friend of mine described it like watching a library burn to the ground. Destruction and ruin, wasted potential.

The needlessness of the burned-down library, of the addict's wreck, the irrationality of his endless pursuit for relief, and the high price at the end of the road are central to its heartbreak and its deservingness of the word. In recovery literature, alcohol and drugs are described as *the rapacious creditor*, who makes things disappear. Self-respect, money, time, teeth, children, and eventually the addicts themselves. And though in the end you're left with absence, which is worse and better than nothing, which is the root of heartbreak, so often it all begins with the simplest of desires—a dream of anesthetization, a final defense against fear.

WHEN THE TEXAS HORNED LIZARD FEELS THREATENED, it shoots blood out of its eye sockets, a tactic that surprises and disgusts its predators, usually coyotes or bobcats, so completely that they run away. But in the process, the lizard can lose up to a third of the blood in its body.

The hairy frog takes a more direct approach to defending itself, making a weapon of its own bones. Also known as the "horror frog," when under attack, the *Trichobatrachus robustus* breaks its toe bones and pushes them through the skin of its feet to form claws. After a time, the claws retract and the skin heals over, but not without scars.

In the rain forest of French Guiana, a species of termite relies on self-sacrifice. When the colony faces danger, they send older members—no longer as productive as they used to be—on suicide missions. These elderly workers wear sacks on their backs, which they fill over a lifetime with toxic crystals produced by glands in the abdomen. When mixed with salivary gland secretions, these crystals create a poisonous liquid that blows up their enemies and themselves.

I read about a small variety of deep-sea squid (*Octopoteuthis deletron*) that breaks off the tip of its own arm when threatened and leaves it behind, twitching and glowing in that dark underworld, as a distraction.

What are you willing to lose to save your life?

I GRADUATED FROM LAW SCHOOL ON A SEARING DAY, OVER ninety degrees in the sun. There was no shade or shelter over the rows of white plastic chairs in front of the dais. More than two hundred of us were getting diplomas that day, boiling in the spirit of celebration. Our families sat and stood behind us, finding shade where they could, mostly clumped together under the palm trees, plastic water bottles crumpling in sweaty hands.

I was full of memory. Sitting there in the sun, listening to my classmates' names being called and waiting for my own name, thinking about how many names I'd memorized over the past nine quarters, which was what cases became: *Name v. Name*. Plaintiff v. Defendant. ∏ v. Δ. Behind each name, each symbol, a whole life. In the beginning, my notes were full of names, and my case briefs read more like summaries of soap operas than legal principles because the cursory symbols, ∏ and Δ, seemed too reductive. Abbreviations of misfortune, appropriations of collision. I spelled their names out in full.

All four of my professors that first semester of 1L used the Socratic method in class—cold-calling students from a seating chart in front of them—which meant I spent hours that fall obsessively remembering the names of plaintiffs and defendants and dreading the sound of my own name.

When my name was called on graduation day, I walked across the stage, took the diploma, and froze mid-handshake for a picture with the dean. On my way back to my seat, I had to remind myself, as I'd done many times that day, that L wouldn't be there waiting for me at the end of the ceremony. In the final weeks of school, we'd tried to find a way forward but could not. The breakup had the artifice of logistics: I had accepted a job in Washington, D.C., at the Children's Defense Fund, and he had just taken a job in California, a state he loved in his bones, a place that meant freedom for him. We were switching places. But it was more than that. I had the strongest feeling I had to let him go. Even though I still loved him. And that day, at the ceremony, it felt like disassociation, or a weakened sense of presence. Because when you love someone you have to let go, a part of you is always in another place, wherever they are.*

I can't find the picture with the dean now, but I have another from that day—me and my two best friends, cheeks flushed, big smiles. We had gone through a lot in three years. Ahead of us there would be a dozen moves, three weddings, eight pregnancies, a few funerals, a miscarriage, and a child's life-threatening heart condition. So much we didn't yet know.

A week later, I packed my books and clothes again, and I drove across the country alone, with the windows down,

---

* I learned years later that L *was* there—he had come to watch me graduate but didn't want to confuse the day with sadness, so he stayed away, in the back, and I never saw him.

listening to country songs about heartbreak, determined to do something good somewhere else. Determined to fill the space that L's absence left in my life.

NATURAL DISASTERS (ACTS OF GOD) ARE ALSO MASTER disappearers. Houses swallowed whole or sucked into the sky. When a big one hits, *heartbreak* pops up in the headlines for days after.

HEALING AFTER TORNADO HEARTBREAK

DESTRUCTION AND HEARTBREAK AS MEXICO REELS FROM EARTHQUAKE

STORM LEAVES BLACKOUTS AND HEARTBREAK

The same themes pertain—destruction and loss—but here it's more than losing; it's having it taken, blown away, washed away, ripped out from under you, ripped from your arms by a riptide. Natural disaster discloses our powerlessness to stop what can hurt us.

Plague feels like one of the most unnatural of natural disasters, provoked, some think, at least in part by swings in climate. Over the past five years, *heartbreak*'s height of usage (by more than 50 percent) was March 2020, just as the coronavirus was beginning to cast its shadow beyond China. Or just as we were starting to see the shadow.

CORONAVIRUS HEARTBREAK: 5-YEAR-OLD GIRL DIES AFTER TWO WEEKS ON VENTILATOR

HEARTBREAK, PRAYER AND MOURNING: US LEADS WORLD
IN CORONAVIRUS DEATHS AFTER DEADLIEST WEEK

During weeks of quarantine, *absence* was the watchword. The streets emptied out. Schools and places of worship shut their doors. Losing strength, losing breath, lost lives. Some reveled in isolation, but most began to drown in it. And then, as the markets tumbled, there were the disappearing jobs.

Recession often follows natural disaster, descending like a second wave of ruin. Its primary verb is also *take*, so *heartbreak* doubles down. The word's highest peak in the news over the past fifteen years—50 percent greater than even March 2020—was in April 2008, the eve of a collapse bested only by the Great Recession.

Heartbreak's popularity in times of great taking reveals the essence of a broken heart—what it is to have and then not have. From Dante's Sonnet IX: *My heart, as with an earthquake, then is cleft, / Which makes my pulse leave all its life behind*.

But unlike other heartbreak, disasters, natural and man-made, are collective. Private loss wrapped up in something shared. This can, though doesn't always, give you something even as it takes away. In *A Paradise Built in Hell*, Rebecca Solnit writes:

> *In the wake of an earthquake, a bombing, or a major storm, most people are altruistic, urgently en-*

gaged in caring for themselves and those around them. . . . When all the ordinary divides and patterns are shattered, people step up—not all, but the great preponderance—to become their brothers' keepers. And that purposefulness and connectedness bring joy amid death, chaos, fear, and loss.

Loss that's shared can make recovery redemptive. This is the unwanted gift that's *possibly* waiting at the center of any heartbreak. The breaking and falling apart offer the chance to come together in some new way, with some new belief of what's possible. *Horrible in itself*, Solnit writes, *disaster is sometimes a door back into paradise, the paradise at least in which we are who we hope to be, do the work we desire, and are each our sister's and brother's keeper.*

But despite the back door that might be waiting at the center of loss, I would never willingly forge ahead to find out. No matter; we're not given a chance to choose.

PEOPLE USED TO THINK INSANITY WAS CAUSED BY EVIL. Possession—is possession a having or a taking?—was a battle between good and evil, and the body and mind were the battlegrounds. For centuries, across cultures, any kind of emotional or mental disturbance was understood as the work of evil spirits and demons. This resulted in treating people by performing exorcisms and burning them at the stake if all else failed.

It's a connection that lingers. In a recent interview, the American spiritualist Caroline Myss says:

> In that same way, when you're going into just, "Well, this is a therapeutic thing, and this person's obviously just schizophrenic or just . . ." That's inadequate. They may well exhibit schizophrenic behavior, and that may well be true. But the schizophrenia could be the caboose on this train, and the engine could be possession. One of the ways that shows up is schizophrenic behavior. They may well be hearing voices, and those voices could be demonic. It is not just a hallucination. But because you won't go there, you will not contact an exorcist, and you have it in your mind that it's just too sophisticated for this world. Well, it's not. Those things happen. Those things happen.

In its language, at least, the law entertains this notion. Certain crimes are described as *malum in se*, evil in itself (as opposed to crimes *malum prohibitum*, which are wrong because they are illegal). Murder is one of those crimes. *Evil mind* and *evil intent* are other phrases officially associated with the mental state (*mens rea*) required by the law of murder. In the hierarchy of wrongdoing, we deem murder the worst. But I wonder about the religiosity that the word *evil* introduces to the supposedly hyperrational, non-emotional world of law.

I have come to think that when we call murder *evil*, what we are really doing is pushing it into the darkness, into the underworld. It's hard not to see the wish fulfillment here. We need murder to be evil and we need to maintain the belief that we are good, or at least average, at least safe. We need murder to be other, demonic. But murder is, like all violence, historically human, natural. And maybe this is what scares and fascinates us most about it: not that it is outside ourselves, but that it is within.

What if the law isn't wrong? Again, I am not talking about logic or science; I am talking about feeling. Evil is how what Scott did *felt*, so maybe the law's use of the word is onto something.

Referring to her abusive girlfriend in her memoir *In the Dream House*, Carmen Maria Machado writes, Evil *is a powerful word. You use it once, and it tastes bad: metallic, false. But what other word can you use for a person who makes you feel so powerless?*

There is terrifying power exhibited by a person who takes another's life. It's godlike.

In any case, back then and sometimes even now, I felt and feel afraid of the idea and the word itself. I was afraid that saying the murder felt *evil* would call it in, turn it up.

Scott's father had been a pastor for a time before the murder.

When my father called my cousin John to tell him what had happened, John said, *Why is it always the preachers' kids?*

This colloquial wisdom—that the children of pastors are often bedeviled—feels Southern but in fact isn't limited by geography. In Eugene O'Neill's play *The Iceman Cometh*, which is set in New York, the main character, Hickey (a pastor's son), says about himself, *Ministers' sons are sons of guns.* He says this just before he confesses to murdering his wife. At the end of the play, a court finds him not guilty by reason of insanity.

It might be a misperception, a matter of unmet expectations: pastors' kids are supposed to be good, so we notice when they're not and that makes it feel frequent. But anecdotal evidence—a common and pervasive experience—often points to something true. And anecdotally, those who've known it to be true whisper about evil. Evil testing the faith of people, pastors and preachers, whose faith is supposed to be strong. Others more rooted in science point to the pressure exerted on the children of pastors to be good. In either case, the story is about pressure that produces a break.

BEFORE FRIDA KAHLO WAS BORN, HER FATHER PAINTED their home bright blue to ward off evil spirits. It's still blue today, and now it's called the Casa Azul, home to the Frida Kahlo Museum. In between her birth and the founding of the museum, it's where she lived with her husband, the painter Diego Rivera, one source of the ceaseless heartbreak dramatized in several of her self-portraits.

These self-portraits, the critic Peter Schjeldahl writes in *The New Yorker*, are not *great art, but they are moving testaments of a great artist*. And though the reproductions we see online and in books and on postcards are bright and vibrant, awash with primary colors, the real paintings themselves, he writes, are *matte and grayish, drinking and withholding light*. This makes a kind of sense; the content is heavy, absorbing, literally consuming.

Kahlo painted many hearts, often broken or maimed. In one of her most famous portraits, *The Two Fridas* (1939), imagined just after her divorce, two Fridas sit side by side, holding hands. Both women gaze out beyond the realm of the painting, toward us or past us. Both have their hearts exposed in their chests. The two hearts are connected by a threadlike vein. The Frida on the right is holding a small picture of Rivera and has a healthy heart. This is the one Rivera loved, Kahlo explained. But the Frida on the left holds a pair of scissors and has a heart full of holes. There is blood on her white lace dress.

Memory, the Heart (1937), Kahlo said, is about the affair Rivera had with her younger sister, Cristina. A huge bloody heart lies slumped on the shore, a trail of blood stretched behind it as if it had been dragged down to the beach. That's the background. In the foreground, Kahlo paints herself floating in the air, that same plaintive stare, but this time with tears on her cheeks. She has a hole in her chest that we can see the sky through, and a long rod shot through the hole. On either end of the rod, a tiny Cupid sits, as if on a seesaw. The woman has no arms. She is flanked by a schoolgirl uniform on one side and a Tehuana dress on the other.

In *The Broken Column* (1944), Kahlo's body is split open to reveal a crumbling pillar instead of organs. In *The Wounded Deer* (1946), her face is superimposed on a deer's body, lying in the forest, shot through with nine arrows. Blood pours from the wounds.

These paintings, and more like them, Schjeldahl writes, belong

> to a category of images with which Kahlo confronted and endured episodes of agony, including heartbreak and rage. (Most piercing are laments of her disastrous pregnancies; she longed for children but physically could not bring a baby to term.)

The paintings are unflinching, both in the gaze of the self-portraiture as well as the blood, the reckoning with pain. Schjeldahl writes:

> Much that is hurt and disappointed in me feels momentarily allayed, and almost healed, when I am in the spell of her art. . . . [H]er self-portraits assure me of two things: first, that things are worse than I know, and, second, that they're all right.

An interviewer once asked Anne Carson, who had recently published the collection *Nox* (an elegy) after the death of her estranged brother, if writing the book helped her understand her brother. Carson said:

> *I finally decided that understanding isn't what grief is about. Or laments. They're just about making something beautiful out of the ugly chaos you're left with when someone dies.*

Kahlo's portraits, too, don't seem interested in understanding, but are instead devoted to expression, which, through their honesty, ends up making something beautiful.

AT FIRST I WANTED TO UNDERSTAND HEARTBREAK AND this thing that happened in my family and the way it shaped my sight, backward and forward. That was what I thought this book would be about. But as time goes on, and through the act of writing, I've come to see that understanding, as a goal, is not much more than a red herring. And that the deeper longing underneath the research is for *making*.

IN TERMS OF MAKING, IN THE HIGHEST COURTROOMS of the land, we're not really making justice, not consistently. We're making laws.

In the recording of the oral arguments of *Miller v. Alabama* (2011), the first words you hear are Chief Justice John Roberts inviting Bryan Stevenson to begin, as if he were calling on him in class. *Mr. Stevenson*, he says.

Stevenson is there to argue the unconstitutionality of juvenile LWOP for all crimes. His clients are Evan Miller and Kuntrell Jackson, both fourteen years old when they committed crimes that sent them to prison for the rest of their lives.*

He moves deftly, invoking *Graham* out of the gate, arguing that the court's reasoning in that case should not be crime-specific. (Remember, *Graham* banned juvenile LWOP sentences for nonhomicide crimes.)

But he doesn't get far. Justice Ruth Bader Ginsburg is the first to interrupt, and the other justices continue to interrupt, in brief and regular intervals, from this point on. It feels like a

---

* *Miller v. Alabama*, 567 U.S. 460 (2012): Evan Miller, from Moulton, Alabama, beat his neighbor, Cole Cannon, with a baseball bat and then set fire to his trailer. Cannon had just sold drugs to Miller's mom, and then invited Miller and a friend back to his trailer, where they drank and smoked. Cannon woke up to see Miller stealing money from his wallet, at which point, Miller's friend hit Cannon with a baseball bat. Miller then took over, throwing a sheet over Cannon's head and hitting him with his fists and the bat, and saying, *I am God. I have come to take your life.*

Kuntrell Jackson, along with two other friends, planned to rob Movie Magic in Blytheville, Arkansas. Jackson stayed outside until the very end, at which point he walked in to see his friend Derrick Shields pull out a sawed-off .410-gauge shotgun on the movie store clerk, Laurie Troup, and shoot her in the face.

volley. They ask questions that take apart his argument in order to see what it's made of. Stevenson flexes his moral clarity.

SONIA SOTOMAYOR: Is it your view that life—a mandatory life without parole for someone like a juvenile is grossly disproportionate?

BRYAN A. STEVENSON: It is, for the very reasons that the Court articulates in both *Roper* and *Graham*. We're not arguing that life without parole is disproportionate to the crime of aggravated murder. We're arguing that the status of children, with all of the deficits that childhood status creates, make that kind of judgment cruel.

Some of the justices seem keen on getting him to misspeak, backing him into a corner. They keep asking him to write the decision for them. *How would you write it?* they ask. *How would you write this decision?* Justice Scalia doesn't hide his disavowal of the notion that these sentences are unusual or cruel.

ANTONIN SCALIA: Well, I thought that modern penology has abandoned that rehabilitation thing, and they—they no longer call prisons reformatories or—or whatever, and punishment is the—is the criterion now. Deserved punishment for crime.

Leave it to Scalia to coolly discard in one breath "that rehabilitation thing," as if it weren't one of the chief rationales of the entire system.*

BRYAN A. STEVENSON: Well, I—I—no.

I think it would still be relevant, Justice Scalia, but—but I also don't think that correctional facilities have identified themselves as having no role to play in the rehabilitative process.

I mean, one of the problems with this sentence of life imprisonment without parole is that it actually bans and shields this population from a whole range of services that are specifically designed to rehabilitate: education services, treatment services, anger management programs.

All of these programs exist within prisons, including the federal prisons, because we do care how people perform when they are released.

And so, corrections is still very much the heart and soul of what we do.

But even if it wasn't [*beautiful pivot*], punishment nonetheless has to be proportionate, and recognize that it can be excessive. And what this Court

---

* As far as I know, law students still learn four rationales for criminal justice when they get to law school: incapacitation, retribution, deterrence, and rehabilitation.

has said is that when you're looking at children, to equate the failings of a child and an adult would be cruel.

It would be unfair to—given our knowledge and understanding of what developmental science has taught us and what we know about kids.

Scalia disagrees with Stevenson, and he never intended to change his mind. But you can hear the other justices struggling. There is a tension developing between what they see Stevenson asking for—this total ban of *all* juvenile life sentences—and a more moderate path they wish he would walk. They want him to ask for less. A more measured approach, the end to *mandatory* life sentences.

A mandatory sentence is one that's cooked into the law. For example, in Louisiana, somebody who's convicted of first-degree murder gets a minimum of life without parole, no matter what. The sentence automatically follows the crime, and the trier of fact (judge or jury) has no discretion to suggest a different one, based on the offender's age, potential to change, or mitigating circumstances, such as the brutal childhood he may have been surviving. Stevenson's client, Evan Miller, had been in and out of foster care his entire life and had attempted suicide four times. Four times by the age of fourteen.

When the justices push for a less drastic approach, Stevenson stands his ground.

BRYAN A. STEVENSON: My preferred rule would be a categorical ban [of LWOP] on all juveniles under the age of eighteen. And I don't want to retreat from that in any way. All of these deficits, all of these characteristics that we're talking about, have been recognized to apply to all youth up until the age of eighteen.

But they keep pressing. Later, Justice Kennedy seems frustrated:

ANTHONY M. KENNEDY: Well, again, it seems you're just forcing us into a—a bipolar position. We're either going to say that you can't prevail at all or that everyone under eighteen is—cannot get life without parole. I don't see this middle course—

BRYAN A. STEVENSON: Yes.

ANTHONY M. KENNEDY: —which you seem to have abandoned, and you can't tell me how a judge would apply it if we—if we chose not to abandon it.

BRYAN A. STEVENSON: Well, I—I don't intend to abandon it, Justice Kennedy.

And then he does what they wanted him to do. He charts a course down the middle.

BRYAN A. STEVENSON: I mean, obviously, I'm arguing for this categorical ban, but I think the Court could obviously do something else.

We think that there is a basis for concluding, unquestionably, that a child under the age of fifteen should not be exposed to life without parole based on this Court's precedents and on the data that's presented.

The Court could set a categorical line there and, at the same time, make a determination that subjecting any child under the age of eighteen to life without parole where there is no ability to consider age is fundamentally at odds with what this Court has now constitutionally recognized in both *Roper* and *Graham*.

When the Court hands down their decision in June, nine days after my graduation, this is exactly what they do: they rule that it's the *mandatory* nature of Miller's and Jackson's sentences that is unconstitutional, not the sentences themselves.

Justice Kagan, who wrote the majority opinion, grounded her logic in how teenagers are different from grown-ups, an assertion proven not only by "common sense—on what 'any parent knows,'" but also "science and social science." And she argued that the decision was consistent with *Graham* and *Roper*, thereby rooting the decision in precedent:*

> The mandatory penalty schemes at issue here . . .
> prevent the sentencer from considering youth and
> from assessing whether the law's harshest term of
> imprisonment proportionately punishes a juvenile
> offender. This contravenes Graham's (and also Roper's)
> foundational principle: that imposition of a State's
> most severe penalties on juvenile offenders cannot
> proceed as though they were not children.

The ruling was celebrated as a victory. In many ways, it was: the decision struck down twenty-nine different state laws that mandated LWOP sentences for juveniles, including Louisiana's.

When I first saw the headlines, I was packing boxes in California, getting ready to move. For a moment, for less

---

* Precedent binds a court to previous decisions, through the principle of *stare decisis*, thereby creating continuity among different courts, years, and facts on a similar question of law. *Black's Law Dictionary* defines *precedent* as a "rule of law established for the first time by a court for a particular type of case and thereafter referred to in deciding similar cases." A court can overrule its own prior decision, relying, for instance, on the notion that our standards of decency evolve. A court can also overrule a lower court's decision. But a lower court cannot overrule a higher court's precedent.

than a minute, I felt a rush of excitement. I thought it might change everything for Scott.

But then I realized how narrow the ruling was. They'd dodged the big question and focused on a technicality. As long as LWOP wasn't automatic, as long as Scott was afforded the chance for a sentencing hearing, it would still be possible for him to get life without parole. It was still likely.

I sat on my bed and scanned the majority opinion, published on the Court's website, for indicators of more revolutionary decisions to come. Justice Kagan wrote:

> Given all we have said in Roper, Graham, *and this decision about children's diminished culpability and heightened capacity for change, we think appropriate occasions for sentencing juveniles to this harshest possible penalty will be uncommon.*

Uncommon felt like a meager offering. What did that even mean? It would be up to prosecutors and judges to decide what *uncommon* meant, which, in Louisiana, meant the decision wouldn't carry much water. Striking down the mandatory-sentencing scheme was necessary, and a victory, but continuing to allow the sentence with loose guidance on how often it should be applied wouldn't mean anything for Scott.

When I listen to the arguments now, so many years later,

the moment that hits me is when Stevenson tells the judges how to decide the case more narrowly. When he tells them how to write it. I keep thinking of this moment and it reminds me of a quote from the novel *My Name Is Lucy Barton* by Elizabeth Strout:

I feel almost, then, that I can hear within me the sound of my own heart breaking, the way you could hear outside in the open air—when the conditions were exactly right—the corn growing in the fields of my youth. I have met many people, even from the Midwest, who tell me that you cannot hear the corn growing, and they are wrong.

In the oral arguments, I can hear something like heartbreak over the recording, but I'm not sure whose heartbreak it is. Stevenson's, maybe, because he likely knew his concession was going to lose the bigger fight. Or maybe the hearts of those in prison who wouldn't have a chance—no room for them down such a narrow way—whole prisons full of breaking hearts, whole fields full, projected into the courtroom.

THE FIRST TIME I MET BRYAN STEVENSON WAS AT A board meeting at the Children's Defense Fund. By this time, I was living in D.C., renting an apartment on Capitol Hill.

Every morning and night I walked past the Capitol, through Stanton Park, and down Massachusetts Avenue past Union Station. After the meeting, as he put on his coat and headed toward the door, I stopped him in the lobby because I didn't want to miss any more chances to say thank you to people who changed my life. *I heard you speak at Stanford*, I said. *It's why I'm here now.* He was kind and warm. He shook my hand and thanked me for telling him.

A few weeks later, President Barack Obama was elected for a second term. I spent Election Day driving people to the polls. I picked up one family—three Black women, three generations voting for the first time. And a month later, in December, in Newtown, Connecticut, Adam Lanza killed twenty-six children and teachers, his mother, and himself.

I was in my office in D.C. when I heard the news. It was morning. Without thinking, I picked up the phone and called one of the top gun safety organizations in the country and asked to speak to their policy director. When I told him who I was and where I was calling from, he said, *Wow, I'm so sorry, what a day for you guys.*

I balked, at first, at his literalism—on a day that many children were murdered, we at the Children's Defense Fund had failed our mandate. But I managed to say, *Yeah, you, too.* And then, in the brief silence that fell between us, I felt suddenly as if I was standing too close to a stranger.

Then I asked, *So what are you guys going to do?* And we starting talking strategy, what to push for on the Hill, what might feasibly get passed. If our haste was a moral misstep, callous and calculated, I didn't care. The Children's Defense Fund had been talking about children and guns for decades.* What had been missing was political will. Gun homicides are the leading cause of death for Black children, and a Black child is fourteen times more likely to die by gunfire than a white child. But now it was middle-class and upper-middle-class, mostly white children in a suburban town in Connecticut, killed all at once, on the same day, in a matter of moments. The kind of thing America might care about (since America has made it clear it doesn't care about Black and brown children). Nothing like this had ever happened before. And I felt an urgent desire, like hunger, to ride the terrible wave to a new shore—a legal landscape that at the very least made it harder, or even impossible, to own a semiautomatic weapon. Harder or even impossible to kill so many children in so little time. Harder to kill so many Black children over such a long and unsung time.

Was it callous? Is this what's wrong with Washington—this impulse to seize the moment of tragedy for political gain? Maybe. But I know that you can pray for grieving families and fight for policies that would have protected those families at the same time.

---

* CDF puts out a report on children and guns every year. The 2019 report found that in 2017, 3,410 children and teens were killed with guns—the greatest number of child and teen gun deaths since 1998.

I was sure new laws would pass.

These kinds of legislative efforts have always relied on the voices of the bereaved, on the human articulation of preventable loss. And in those days, as I worked with parents who'd put their children's bodies in the ground because they'd been killed at Sandy Hook or Virginia Tech or in the circadian violence of Chicago, I thought and tried not to think of the parents of the child Scott killed. When I saw Adam Lanza's face on the news, hollowed-out and ghostlike, I thought of Scott's mug shot. The annihilative wish against themselves, turned outward.

Around this time, I got a letter from L in the mail. He wrote to tell me he still loved me. It felt like finding something I thought I'd lost. A few weeks later, he came to visit, and we spent a night talking in my tiny studio apartment. I told him I was sure that gun safety legislation would pass. *I am sure*, I said. *It just has to*. He read out loud from the Yeats's *Collected Works* we'd found earlier at a used bookstore, and the Duraflame log crackled, providing little heat or light. We decided, that night, to try to figure out a way to be together.

On New Year's Eve, at a friend's mother's house, we gathered around the kitchen island to write down one thing we believed would happen in the new year. I wrote down *gun laws* and threw it into the bowl, along with everyone else's scrap-paper hopes and predictions.

———————

THE COVERAGE OF SANDY HOOK WAS FILLED WITH *heartbreak*.

GRIEF AND HEARTBREAK FROM THE
CONNECTICUT ELEMENTARY SCHOOL MASSACRE

UNSPEAKABLE TERROR AND HEARTBREAK

SANDY HOOK ELEMENTARY: HEARTBREAK AS
FUNERALS CONTINUE ALL WEEK

The coverage of mass shootings (another unnatural disaster) always is, but this one especially. This one played out in a kindergarten classroom, in the hallways of a school, under desks and inside cubbies, with construction paper and glue and drawings on the wall. Meanwhile, parents gathered in a room at the nearby fire station, waiting to take their children home. A lesson you learn quickly as a parent and come to rely on: your fear is unfounded. What a terrible unlearning that must be.

In the news, even milder stories with children at the center are described in terms of heartbreak. It has to do with innocence, but also with the ferocity of parents' love. *Your heart outside your body.* This is how people sometimes describe your child. Your whole heart, breakable and tottering away from you. Among the Shakespearean characters who die of heartbreak, most die of a sorrow connected to their children: Lady Montague in *Romeo and Juliet*; Brabantio, Desdemona's father, in *Othello*; Gloucester in *King Lear*; and of course Lear himself. God chose to understand human suffering, the story goes, not through unrequited love or illness or pain, but through the death of his son.

In the midst of all this, I wrote to Bryan Stevenson, asking for help with Scott's case. Looking not for representation, but for guidance about how he would suggest navigating the changing sentencing landscape after *Miller* and *Jackson*. Those cases invalidated the laws on the books for charging and sentencing Scott. I wondered if there was a way in which this moment of uncertainty might serve Scott's cause. I wrote:

> *Because of your incredible victories in the Supreme Court, there is no longer any law under which Scott can be sentenced in LA. The defense attorney submitted a motion to delay trial until the state legislature has amended the state code to reflect* Miller *and* Jackson, *but the judge denied it. So if they proceed to trial and Scott is convicted, he will have to wait for a sentence and will likely be transferred to an adult prison while he waits. I'm just trying to make sense of this—why we would proceed to convict someone without an appropriate sentence on the books— and wondered if you had any insight, or had similar difficulty in the application of* Miller *and* Jackson

elsewhere? If there is anyone you think it might be helpful to talk with, please let me know.

This is what he wrote me back:

I'm glad you reached out to me about your cousin. I think the attorney can argue that the judge has the authority to impose a sentence that creates a meaningful possibility of release. I would use the absence of a legal way to impose LWOP as a basis to eliminate that sentence as an option and then either negotiate through settlement discussions an acceptable sentence or ask the judge to impose a sentence that is currently available. We made these arguments successfully in some of the Graham cases in Louisiana. The Court could impose the 20/45 sentence which requires 20 years or parole eligibility at age 45 sentence or hopefully something more favorable in light of the mental illness. However, I wouldn't probably want to wait for the legislature to act on this because they are likely to endorse an alternative sentence which is worse than 20/45.

He also connected me with an attorney at a juvenile justice organization in Louisiana, and I talked to her the next day.

And the day after that, Scott dropped his insanity defense and pled guilty to second-degree murder.

And that was it. That day he lost his chance for anything but a life sentence.

Though I now see my arrogance, back then, it felt like Scott was giving up. Of course he accepted the plea to avoid a trial that would have been lengthy and grueling for both families. The odds weren't good, and his attorney couldn't promise the outcome they wanted. The idea of going through it, only to be sentenced to death in prison anyway, felt impossible.

But back then I believed in fighting to the last. It was what I'd learned from watching Bryan Stevenson and Marian Wright Edelman at CDF and the attorneys at NPP and the attorneys at the legal clinic where I'd found a home during law school. I put my chips on moral certainty and fighting.

I still believe these modes are essential in the work of justice. And I still believe it's indicative of a damning flaw that someone should have to give up the only chance he has in order to avoid the pain of a trial. This flaw is the consequence of the system's adversarial setup and the antagonism it breeds. Theatricality and crooked incentives. It's part of the reason that rape victims don't press charges and defendants take pleas they shouldn't take.* I have a friend who was a public defender in Louisiana for ten years, and re-

---

* According to a 2016 Department of Justice report on violent crimes, an estimated 80 percent of sexual assaults go unreported, and in nearly 11 percent of the nation's 349 DNA exoneration cases, innocent people entered guilty pleas.

cently he confessed to a paranoia he still carries that people in his life are deliberately misunderstanding him, twisting his words to mean something else. Because that was what it was like in court. That was what *adversarial* meant. Language was weaponized. The stakes were always high, and the game was rarely fair. There are good prosecutors and good defenders, but everyone is acting inside the confines of a system infected by its own corroding foundations.

When I learned Scott dropped his defense, I felt furious at the system that provoked such an outcome.

And then, a few weeks later, Congress failed to pass any kind of gun reform legislation. Walking home from work that evening, past the Capitol, which glowed at night like something great, like something touting its own greatness on a day it had failed, I felt empty. This is how it can feel to lose—a hollowing. I thought of the parents who'd lost their children on that winter day in Newtown, and how so many of them had channeled their grief straight into activism. What now for them? How would they go on?

AS A NEW MOTHER, LORNI NOTICED HOW, ON CERTAIN nights when she lay down to sleep, she could feel her heartbeat accelerate, quiver, scramble. It happened infrequently, so she didn't worry. It was the only heart she'd ever known. And she had always noticed her heart. As a child, she noticed the way she could speed up or slow down her heartbeat with her breath.

She moved through decades of life with her heartbeat, watching her children grow up and move out of the house, push her away, as children are supposed to, and crash back in—home for the holidays, the tricky heaven of a full house again. Her son Matt worked construction in New Mexico and, after years of struggling with addiction, had finally gotten sober. He was happy, leveled out. Lorni and her husband, Matt's father, went to visit him one summer, and she realized while looking at her son, now in his thirties, clean and going to meetings, that she was the way she was because of him. From the very beginning of his life, she'd formed around her son the way a river pours around a rock. She felt proud of who she was. Grateful for the rock, the struggle.

A few weeks later, Matt was hit by a truck on a construction site and died. Grief, Lorni said, hit her the same way, like a truck, like a punch to her gut that left her breathless and caved in, head down, arms wrapped around her own body as if it might fall apart if she let go. In its less acute moments, as the days passed, she described grief as heaviness. Pressing, pressing, never lifting. Nothing mattered.

After Matt's death, her heartbeat got louder. She could feel it and hear it all the time, like a drum, and the accelerations and flutterings picked up in frequency. In grief, everything had changed in her body, but this change startled her. She started to worry something was wrong.

It took her months to make an appointment—grief eradicating notions of to-do lists, scheduling—but when she finally went in to see her doctor and get some tests done, the doctor was worried enough to refer her to a cardiologist. Lorni asked to see the report, but the paragraphs of text stared back at her, defying understanding. Words like *fibrillation* and *arrhythmia*, clusters of acronyms.

The first cardiologist she saw told her that the patterns of her heartbeat indicated an increased chance for atrial fibrillation, which could lead in turn to blood clots, stroke, and heart failure. She mentioned Matt's death and wondered if that might have something to do with it, but the cardiologist said it wasn't related. He offered no words of consolation. Bringing up Matt in that cold office made her cry. The cardiologist told her to follow up in three months. When she made the follow-up appointment, she asked to see the *other* cardiologist at the practice.

This second cardiologist was better. He walked her through each word of the heart testing she'd done. He told her he was not worried, that there was no reason for her to be either. When she mentioned her grief, he said it was possibly related. *We cannot rule it out*, he said. She walked away feeling like grief was *the mercy of a word* she'd been looking for. Her heart started to settle down.

Studies have shown a connection between irregular heartbeat and heartbreak. Danish researchers conducted a study in 2016 that found cardiac arrhythmia is 41 percent more likely in those grieving the loss of a spouse. The more sudden and unexpected the loss, the healthier the grieved and griever, the more likely an irregular heartbeat. And this tracks with the anecdotal evidence of heart doctors. Commenting on the study, Dr. Mark Estes, the director of the New England Cardiac Arrhythmia Center at Tufts Medical Center, said: *This really validates prior observations. It's something we hear from our patients all the time.*

But no one is certain exactly why. It might be hormones—stress hormones, like adrenaline, which cause inflammation and can interfere with lots of normal bodily processes, including the heart's. One of the study's authors pointed to how *mental stress* takes a toll on the autonomic nervous system, which regulates the electrical nerve pathways that trace through the heart to the muscle, enabling a contraction of the heart chambers.

This medical language is metaphorical, grasping at something just out of reach. It tries to describe with images and systems and symbols something so far unseeable.

One thing science can see: the pattern of electricity that's responsible for an abnormally fast heartbeat looks like a spiral. It's called Spiral Wave Re-entry. *Spiral waves are ubiquitous in nature*, writes Dr. Sandeep Jauhar, *so it is no surprise that this pattern is seen in the heart as well.* Other spiral waves include cold air through smoke, aggregates of amoebas, hurricanes, dark matter in the universe, and the way water moves around and over stones—the very same way Lorni described being shaped by her son, like water around a rock.

I met Lorni for the first time just after Matt died, so I've only known her heartbroken. She lives in Vermont, near my parents, and I've grown close to her daughter, Liza, Matt's sister, a writer and mother to a toddler. Talking to Lorni now, three years since Matt's death, in a coffee shop on a cold, bright day just before the solstice, I can tell she's stronger now than she was when I met her, that she's surviving. And I remember what Bonnie Gorscak said about how we're built to move through grief. Lorni is moving through. She looks clearer, somehow, less fragile. Her hair is almost white in the sun and her eyebrows are dark brown and her bright green eyes twinkle when she talks about her granddaughter, Quinn. She cries only once, which is markedly different from before, when she couldn't talk about Matt without crying.

Now the crying comes when she mimics the posture she used to fall into, in the early days, when a wave of grief would come and leave her breathless. In the coffee shop, she's showing me how she used to fall into her body, her head cradled in both hands, her chest carved out and hollow, and as she acts out the posture, it triggers the tears almost like a reflex, because her body remembers. The heart knows what it means to drop into the carved-out cavity, even as it's also gotten stronger, even as electric waves still spiral for brief moments, like a tiny galaxy inside her, like water around a rock.

———

I GAVE MY NOTICE IN THE SUMMER AFTER SANDY HOOK.
L flew east, and we packed my car and drove west together
for a second time, across the middle of the country. We
stopped in Colorado and drove to the top of a mountain
twelve thousand feet above sea level and watched elk eating
grass along the rocky peak. The clouds looked close enough
to touch.

In California, we moved into the bright shoebox apartment in the Castro. Meanwhile, in Louisiana, Scott awaited
sentencing.

I learned the outcome of the hearing after it was over,
when my father called and left it in a message: *Hi, it's me. I
was just calling to tell y'all that Scott was sentenced to life
in prison without parole. Which is heartbreaking and just
what they were afraid of. Call me back if you want to talk.
Love you.*

It was too late to call him back when I heard the message, but I opened my computer and Googled Scott's name.
A picture came up of him wearing a black-and-white-striped
jumpsuit, his hair close cut, older, bigger.

I skimmed the coverage on *The Advocate* and *Feliciana
Today*, swallowing quotes and facts in chunks that were hard
to swallow, and then scrolling to the end of the article and
then going back to the beginning to read it, more carefully,
again. I learned things as I read that I hadn't known.

I didn't know that in the weeks and months or maybe
even years leading up to his arrest, Scott's thinking had

started to unravel. To depart from shared reality. He'd started to believe that no one liked him, and even though he had friends, he imagined himself alone. He believed something was wrong with him. He'd started watching a television show about a vigilante serial killer who murders bad guys, and he'd started to identify with the killer, who feels better after he kills. He started to believe that whatever was wrong with him, too, could be explained, appeased, only by killing. He decided that he was meant to be a killer.

The clinical word for these unravelings is *delusions*. In their testimony, the experts used the words *delusions* and *delusional* often, but there was no consensus as to a legally recognizable diagnosis. Some described a *psychotic episode*. Dr. Claybourne, who interviewed Scott just after the murder, called him *an abnormal teen* with *a superior intellect* and *an IQ between 120 and 129*.

Each expert also described Scott's confusion after the murder, his unmet expectations. He'd expected to feel relief but didn't.

Dr. Claybourne testified that Scott wondered if he did it again differently, *perhaps to a female*, if he would have found the relief he was hoping for.

Perhaps to a female.

I slammed the computer shut. I went to sleep that night in California, a million miles away, and dreamed about a baby who could speak in full sentences, whom I was supposed to be taking care of but kept losing.

The next morning, the sun streamed through our windows and I opened the computer and picked up where I left off. *Most people feel guilt, and that inhibits them from doing it again*, said Dr. Sandburg, the psychiatrist appointed by the state. *It isn't the doing of wrong that worries me . . . good people do wrong things. It is just how we process those things afterwards.*

Ryan's mother's therapist took the stand to read a statement on her behalf. In a trial, this is called victim impact testimony. Her therapist said she wanted the courtroom to know that Ryan wasn't unsupervised, that he was right ahead of her, that he was just *in the wrong place at the wrong time*. She wanted everyone to know that *there was nothing she could have done, regardless of how much medical equipment she may have had with her. Ryan's neck was practically severed, except for his spine*. She wanted the sentencing judge to know that she believes Scott is *a threatening individual and the idea of him being eligible for parole is frightening to her*.

When it was Ryan's grandfather's turn, he asked to give Scott a picture of Ryan to look at:

> *I want you to stare at that picture . . . because you will see that face when you wake up each morning, at times during the day, and before you go to sleep for the rest of your life. This is the curse that I put on*

you. . . . He was a little boy who loved life. . . . Every day was an adventure for him. The devastation you caused my family will heal eventually, but a scar will always be there. The hole you created in our hearts is filled with all the wonderful memories. . . . I don't hate you anymore, but I will never forgive you. That's not my job. That belongs to someone other than me. After today, I will close the chapter on you. You will not exist in our family's world. It is my hope that if you ever do leave prison, it will be feetfirst in a pine box.

Then Ryan's father, who asked for the maximum sentence. Then Scott himself. Reporters described Scott as rocking back and forth in his chair and taking deep breaths. He started with apologies:

I'm so sorry. I'm so sorry. I've tried to understand how bad I hurt you all these years. I'm sorry. I'm really sorry. He didn't deserve this. He was innocent. He didn't do anything to me. I hurt you so bad and I'm so sorry. I was all twisted up inside and crazy. I was miserable all the time. I didn't feel like I could do anything. I didn't have a reason to do anything. I hated myself. There was nothing good about me. I couldn't talk to anyone. I dreaded trying to communicate. I wanted so bad to just have friends but I couldn't do it. I'd just walk around by myself and I thought if people saw me they'd think I was going to meet someone. No one ever noticed I was alone. . . . I didn't want anyone to know the thoughts that were in my head. They'd hate me if they knew the thoughts in my head, but . . . now you all know and now you do all hate me. . . . I didn't have any right to feel so bad. That doesn't make up for killing a little boy. I tried to keep my feelings in my head and just wait for them to go away. . . . I'd watch movies or do extra credit to distract myself. I watched so many movies about murder and I felt similarities with the murderers. I just knew that had to be significant. I really felt like I was that kind of person. They all felt how I felt. I thought I had to be like them to feel successful. The only thing they did that I didn't do was kill people. My only thought all the time was that I had to kill somebody. It doesn't make sense, I know. I didn't have a choice. I couldn't breathe if I didn't do it. It was like it was meant to be. Fated. You don't get to choose what kind of person you are. I wouldn't have these kinds of thoughts if I weren't really this kind of person. . . . The second it happened, I wanted to take it back. I know I'm not a serial killer. I know I'm not really that kind of person. I know myself better now. I couldn't do it again. I can't hurt another family. I can't hurt my family again. . . . I'd kill myself to bring him back. I wish I were dead. Now I pray a lot. I just want to start my time and try to be normal. Sane. I don't know what to do now. It's too much. It's too big. It's twisted up and crazy. I don't know how I could do this. It wasn't me. I killed your son and I'm sorry. I'm so sorry.

Then Ryan's grandmother yelled out, into the courtroom, "Look at us when you speak!" And Scott raised his head to meet her eyes:

I'm sorry. I'm so sorry. I'd do anything to take it back. I hope God helps you somehow because there is nothing more I can do. The only thing that makes it better is knowing that he is in heaven. I should be in hell.

When Scott's lawyer asked him if he thought he could be normal again, he said:

I hope so, but I don't know if I deserve to be. I should have just killed myself before I hurt him. I don't know if I have anything that I could contribute [to society]. I just know I want to be better. I just want to be a good Christian where I can face God.

Then the prosecutor asked him what would happen if he got out, and he said:

I don't want to get out until I go to hell.

Then the prosecutor asked him what happened that day, and Scott answered:

I attacked him because he was weaker than me. I'm a weak person. I cut up both my knees while I was kneeling over him because he was fighting so hard. . . . I'm ashamed. I stood by the trail and just waited for him to go by. Nothing was going through my mind . . . it was just actions. . . . I told the doctors and the police the truth about what I was feeling at the time, but that's not how I feel anymore. It changes. The truth changes.

Then Abe, Scott's father, took the stand. At the end of his testimony, he turned to Scott and spoke to him directly:

Whatever happens and wherever you go, I'll never abandon you. I'll never stop loving you. I'm your dad. I'll never give up on you or believe that your life story is over. We'll make this life journey together wherever it goes.

When it was time for the judge to announce his sentence, he said it was the hardest part of his job to deprive someone of their freedom. And then he spoke to Ryan's family about the limits of the law to make things right:

*I wish that whatever I do would make you feel better,
but it won't. . . . I suspect when you leave here, you
won't feel much better than when you came in. The
system that brings us here today is a good system,
and it works, but it's not very good at easing the pain
of the victims, and I understand that, but that's why
we're here.*

A good system. A system that works. A system that works
at incapacitation, and punishment, but not at rehabilitation
or deterrence—not in cases like these—and it doesn't work
to make things whole. So how good is it? What does it mean
that we continue to punish even as the mechanisms responsible for punishing acknowledge the inability of punishment
to make victims whole or healed?

After his preamble, the judge sentenced Scott to life without parole at Angola. In discussing his rationale, he noted
the lack of diagnosis:

*There is not enough evidence that there is anything
to fix or that can be fixed to prevent this sort of inexplicable crime from happening again. That means
it could happen again.*

Scott had failed the tests the doctors had given him for
sociopath and psychopath. He didn't meet the criteria for
schizophrenia. *Broken* was the word the defense's psychiatrist

used to describe Scott's brain. And this uncertainty around his diagnosis translated to a lack of diagnosis, to *no* diagnosis, which, in the eyes of the law, meant a finding of sanity, which categorized the crime as nothing less than calculated and cold-blooded.

At the bottom of the article covering the hearing, readers left comments praising the judge's decision, and calling Scott "a monster" and "evil":

I hope he rots in his cell.

The only way he's getting out is feetfirst in a casket.

The most recent comment, written four years after the trial, at the very bottom of the page is written by Ryan's grandfather. He writes that losing Ryan *made an empty hole in our hearts that will never heal.* Scott should die in prison, he writes, *whether by his own hand or by another prisoner, if he ever sees one.* He writes how Scott is in solitary confinement and spends twenty-three hours a day in his cell, with one hour allowed for exercise outside in a cage. *I think he should not even be allowed to have that hour.*

THREE MONTHS AFTER THE SENTENCING HEARING, I STARTED teaching at a prison. Twice a week, I drove to San Quentin to teach college-level writing. The class was a prerequisite for a degree program, offering men inside the chance to pursue and eventually earn a BA. You had to have your GED to take the class. There was always a miles-long waitlist to get into the program. This made for easy teaching in many ways—the students' desire to be in the room set them apart from other groups I'd taught. But the teaching was hard because of the need, which was palpable and often felt emotional. Some students, on some days, were quick to feel frustrated—with themselves, with one another, with the work, with me. I was regularly told that I'd spent too much time with one student at the expense of others. Tensions could run high quickly. And sometimes, on some days, I was bad at disentangling myself as these narratives played out.

During teacher training, we were told to be careful and conscious of the way we acted. We were not allowed to wear makeup, no revealing or fitted clothing. I usually wore baggy brown pants and an oversize sweater. When I walked through the gates of the prison, I made an effort to seem like someone who hadn't spent years up until that point courting, accounting for, or deflecting the fact of men looking at me. *Neutralize*, I thought as I walked through the prison yard. I knew how easily narratives of desire can run roughshod over what's meant as politeness, and that is a fact not particular to prison yards.

The rules about boundaries and language were also strict. No touching on the shoulder, no close talking, nothing that could be construed as *something*. And in terms of language, do not say, for instance, *When you do your assignment at home*, because a prison cell is not a home.

Sometimes I made mistakes. One night a man gave me an

envelope with my name on it. And though I shouldn't have accepted it—should have said in the moment, kindly but firmly, *Thank you, but we're not supposed to have any kind of private correspondence*—instead, I took the envelope hurriedly as I said goodbye to everyone and tucked it in with the rest of the class notes, extra handouts, and assignments I'd collected that day. When I opened it that night at home, I found a rambling two-page poem in rhyming couplets. A flag thrown over the line. It had roses and hearts drawn in the margins of the pages like illuminations. It was not explicit or vulgar, just complimentary. The writer described giving me a foot massage. Immediately I searched for my own fault. What had I done to invite this?

I followed the protocols laid out by the program and told the director about the letter, which she asked to see. She then recommended I have a conversation with the student, one on one. She told me to be firm, to tell him why it wasn't okay. I wasn't sure I could, but I didn't tell her that. *Buck up*, I said to myself. As the student and I sat down to talk, I remember feeling we were moving through murky waters, troubled by inequities (prisoner/free, man/woman, Black/white) and the impossibility of perfect boundaries or perfect relationships. All the rules at the prison represented deep anxiety about this impossibility. The talk itself, which took place after class in an office room inside the academic building where I taught, was predictably uncomfortable. But the student didn't press the agenda of the letter. He said he was just trying to be nice because he could tell I was stressed.

When I think of it now, I see that if this man's misstep was trespass, we shared more than we didn't. Where do our stories end and others' begin?

Sometimes I thought of Scott as I walked across the prison yard on my way to class. The yard was always busy with men playing basketball or standing in small groups, talking under a low-slung sun before dusk. I wondered what the sunset looked like from death row in Louisiana.

I HAD KEPT UP SENDING BOOKS. SCOTT WAS REQUESTING anything by Faulkner or Fitzgerald, plus John le Carré. I sent him *Light in August*, *The Beautiful and Damned*, and *The Spy Who Came in from the Cold*.

I picked up my old copy of *The Beautiful and Damned* and found pages of underlined passages. I had been a teenager when I'd read it, just a few years younger than Scott.

> *[Life is] so damned hard, so damned hard . . . it just hurts people and hurts people, until finally it hurts them so that they can't be hurt ever any more. That's the last and worst thing it does.*

I suppose that had seemed true to me when I read it, and some days still did, but I was starting to know I needed another belief. Skipping around, I found another underlined passage:

I don't care about truth. I want some happiness.

I always added a note, like *Merry Christmas* or *Happy birthday*, along with the books I sent to Scott, but I wasn't sure if he ever saw them because I knew the guards might throw them away as they went through the packages in the mailroom.

I loved the golden light lying heavy on those California hillsides as I drove to San Quentin, but I felt the blow of dissonance and chance. I felt it when I had to step over sleeping bodies on the sidewalk to reach the door of our apartment, too, where I had a linen closet full of matching clean sheets, folded in stacks, and a refrigerator full of vegetables, milk, and eggs. I felt it when I got a thank-you note from Scott, carefully handwritten with a pencil on lined paper and folded neatly into the envelope.

Because of Scott's age and crime, he was assigned a cell on death row, a decision purportedly for his own good. Being out in the general population wasn't safe for him. But death row also made him ineligible for services, classes, and groups. Anything like a life as we imagine lives to be, made up of shifting pieces, of schedules and scenery and movement, was impossible. All he had was time. He had been given not a life sentence, but rather a death sentence delayed.

A year in, his counsel appealed the sentence on several grounds, but the circuit court affirmed the lower court's decision. If I had to write a case brief for Scott's appeal, this is how it would look:

Procedural History: Δ charged by grand jury indictment with first-degree murder. Pled not guilty and not guilty by reason of insanity. Then Δ withdrew this plea and pled guilty to second-degree murder. After sentencing hearing, Δ sentenced to LWOP. Δ now appeals, designating five assignments of error.

Judgment: Court affirms lower court conviction and sentence.

Issues:
1. whether trial court failed to take into account Δ's youth in sentencing him to LWOP;

2. whether trial court erred when it gave no weight to evidence of Δ's potential for growth and rehabilitation;

3. whether trial court erred in allowing improper victim impact statements at the sentencing hearing;

4. whether trial court erred in sentencing Δ to harshest sentence available where there was no evidence he was the worst offender;

5. whether Δ's sentence is unconstitutionally excessive.

Holding and rationale: Δ's assignments of error are without merit. Trial court complied with *Miller* and adequately considered the factors set forth in Article 894.1. Based on testimony at the sentencing hearing, the trial court's careful review of the facts, and the nature of the crime ("brutal," "atrocious"), and trial court's included justifications for LWOP sentence, court finds no abuse of discretion. Sentence not grossly disproportionate to the severity of the offense and, therefore, not unconstitutionally excessive.

In their decision, the circuit court wrote: *We find the murder of a small child to be the worst crime and the defendant to be the worst offender. . . . [G]iven the violence and brutality of the crime, the maximum sentence was justified in this case.*

The worst crime, the worst offender.

IN SAN FRANCISCO, I STARTED TO PUBLISH SOME OF MY writing online, some paid and unpaid jobs. Mostly I wrote about prisons and guns and homelessness and the things I saw filling up the world. Then—as happens so often to people who write online—I started getting emails from someone I didn't know who felt they knew me.

In the emails, this person said he could see me and feel me, knew that we were connected. He said he could *taste* my life, see my apartment, knew where I lived. He strung together images that made sense only to him, sentences about tomatoes and blood and sunlight. He signed many of his emails *Love, B.* There were always strange capitalizations and many exclamation points and question marks.

The first person I told about the emails was my friend Caroline, whose father is schizophrenic. He sends her postcards and letters from far away in Great Britain, where he's lived almost her entire life, some of which are benign and some of which are frightening, but all of which convey that particular cadence of a diseased mind. We have talked about it often—this cadence, the rhythms and intonations of someone living in a world of unshared facts—and the way the evidence of disease inspires dis-ease in her. There she is, going about her day, varyingly challenged and beguiled by her own human life, and then a letter from her father, a man she's never known, has the power to topple the structure. Slim and unsettling, a piece of paper rife with disease. Her hands shake; she puts the letter away.

The thing Caroline understood about the emails I got was how physically threatened they made me feel. I had a hard time making sense of this fear because the contact was electronic and invisible. But somehow I feared physical danger. For a few days it felt like B was around every corner. I felt reptilian fear. I was on alert.

Then I stumbled onto a string of Twitter accounts that were talking about me by name. I assumed they were all created by him. Each one had the same voice as the emails. And one day when I was telling someone about it, wishing Twitter would intervene and shut down the accounts, the person reminded me that people who were mentally ill had every right to use the internet, too. Also, they said, mentally ill people were not dangerous.

The part of me that is drawn to absolutes, to moral certainty, sprang to attention. I wanted to adopt both of these opinions as my own. I wanted to be someone who believed this, and who said things like this to other people, because I wanted it to be true and also it's the kind of opinion that marks you as a good person. I have always wanted to be good, and I have always worried I'm not. But in the back of my mind there was Scott, whose mental break had made him not only dangerous but deadly, had caused him to do something that felt like evil.

One of the emails B sent me came through with a name. It turned out this was his real name, and a Google search led me back to where I grew up. I learned he was someone I went to school with. I didn't know him, wouldn't have recognized him on the street, because he was a few years older, but I remembered his brother, who was lovely and lively and played music and did dance and theater. It turns out B was schizophrenic. Through the grapevine I learned he was violent toward his family. He may or may not have lit his family home on fire. They had tried, unsuccessfully, to have him committed. But now he was living in California, under some kind of supervision.

A few years after he stopped emailing me, I learned he was arrested for stalking and assault. Had my fear been misplaced? In my mind, I cast about for the line where his right to use the internet bumped up against my right to feel unafraid. But then I realized that this was not a right I was guaranteed, not legally or otherwise. Being unafraid may be a choice we learn to make over time, but it's not a right. You need only be born a girl with a body that starts to change into a woman's to learn you're not entitled to freedom from physical threat.

So we come up with our own defenses. My defense against B was vigilance, which I'd learned in my body from growing up around fear and anger. It was easy to resuscitate, that old trick of trying to stay safe. The price I paid for this defense took its physical form as sleeplessness and a racing heart. It is harder to quantify the emotional cost.

———

EVEN THE HEART, WHICH IS STRONG, MADE UP OF MOSTLY muscle, defends itself in ways that fail.

The main heartbeat machine inside the heart is called the sinoatrial (SA) node, and it conducts an electrical impulse that moves through the heart and causes it to contract. But if this primary system fails or even falters, there are other parts that jump in to pick up the rhythm. For instance, the atrioventricular (AV) node, located in the middle of the muscle.

Normally, the AV node's job is to slow things down slightly, allowing time for the valves to open and let blood in. But it can also fire and contract the lower chambers of the heart by itself, which it will do if the main system gets in trouble. The point of this backup pacemaker is to delay a failure long enough for the problem to be caught. You might notice an irregular heartbeat, a rhythm that's too fast or slow, and go to the doctor, who will then discover the underlying failure of the SA node.

But sometimes the backup system backfires. Sometimes the AV node hijacks the system and overrides the natural heartbeat unnecessarily, which can cause you to die.

Even the most elegant systems of life don't guarantee life.

PART III

HOW YOUR

HEART POUNDS

INSIDE ME

I think now more than half
Of life is death   but I can't die
Enough for all the life I see

—SHANE MCCRAE,
  "Jim Limber in Heaven Is a
  Nexus at Which the Many
  Heavens of the Multiverse
  Converge"

L and I got married in my parents' backyard on a cold day in October. My father walked me down the aisle, under the honey locust trees, and my mother wrote a short essay on good beginnings that my friend Caroline read at the ceremony. We sang "Amazing Grace" and Aunt Louise said a prayer for us. We kissed, and people threw rice that my mother and I had poured into tiny mesh bags the night before. I wore my grandmother Sharon's wedding dress, Belgian lace with tiny seed pearls sewn in swirling patterns across the back and sleeves. We invited her but she declined, which wasn't surprising. She sent a check instead. But I didn't feel her missing that day. I felt a kind of happiness that I had never felt before, unmatched tenderness and joy. Nothing kept me from happiness that day and night, not the cold or the gray or the loss of people I'd loved or the sadness I'd been filled with in recent years. I was filled with making.

A few months after the wedding, I started writing to Scott, and later talking to him on the phone. This is when I finally started to know him.

I don't remember exactly what day or why I finally put a

letter in the mail. Like many beginnings and endings other than weddings and funerals, this one was not marked by ceremony. I slid into this new chapter of knowing him without consciousness. It was something I'd been meaning to do for years and then one day I finally did it. A culmination of stifled intention.

Our conversations were often about books. After six years of jail and prison, he was the best-read person I knew. One time on the phone I asked him how many books he'd read since being locked up, and he quickly did the math and calculated about 156 books a year, over 900 books total. We talked about the formation of Christianity, about ancient Rome. He told me about his identification with Raskolnikov in *Crime and Punishment*—a story, like Scott's, that doesn't circle around *who* the killer is but *why*, and Dostoyevsky's interest in self-destructive choices, and the precarious balance between choice and choicelessness. At his sentencing hearing, Scott described his crime in terms I'll never forget: he said that he took Ryan's choices away.

After I sent him Neil Gaiman's retelling of Norse mythology, we talked about the Norse gods, and he lit up while talking about Loki and his penchant for mischief. I told him about Bryan Stevenson and sent him *Just Mercy*. He said it was *really great* and lent it to a few others who were on death row with him. Sometimes he told me about his life. Days on death row are entirely determined by who your neighbor is.

He told me that death row turns men into animals. *Boring is good*, he said. It wasn't always boring. Once I got a letter asking for help—*I'm desperate*, he wrote. *Is there anything you can do?* He was trying to get off death row so he could build some kind of life in the land of forever that stretched out before him without parole. Throughout all our conversations, I never asked him about that day in June, the day he walked out of his home and never returned, and I never asked him why.

I NEVER ASKED SCOTT WHY, BUT I DIDN'T STOP THINK-ing about it. Wanting to plumb sense from senselessness is its own kind of defense. I wanted to feel less afraid.

Murder in particular provokes the desire to understand because it is so frightening. People read a story, or hear about something that happened, and look harder and harder to learn why. This, in its simplest form, is what fuels our cultural moment of true crime obsession. Podcasts and Netflix series let you stare as long as you want, offering up the details and stretching out the question of *why* for as long as it will stretch. Consumers scan for differences or similarities among themselves, the killer, and the victim. Some people ask themselves if they're capable of gruesome violence, and some people ask themselves if they are capable of escaping it. Sarah Manguso writes in *300 Arguments*: *I read sad stories to inoculate myself against grief. I watch action movies to identify with the quick-witted heroes. Both the same fantasy: I'll escape the worst of it.*

Dr. Marissa Harrison, an associate professor of psychology at Penn State Harrisburg, said it's about—again—evolution. We evolved to pay attention to things that could harm us so that we can better avoid them: *You would pay attention to, and have interest in, the horrific, because in the ancestral environment, those who "tuned in" to horrible events left more descendants, logically because they were able to escape harmful stimuli.*

Many people, encountering Scott's story for the first time, want to know *why* so they can draw a line in the sand and stand on the other side of it. Parents are particularly quick to do the mental equations of separation. *I would have known if my child was sick, had begun to think of himself as a serial killer, was watching hours and hours of* Dexter. *How could you not see it? How could they have missed it?*

Not far into my son's life, I felt a similar instinct. It was impossible to imagine not knowing him, impossible to imagine letting him slip away. The intimacies of that first year of life, the tie between his moods and mine, my attention to his rhythms. He drank milk from my body and I licked the peanut butter off his fingers. How could I miss it if he started, someday, to unravel? But even now that he's a toddler and leaning into the boundaries of his own personhood, I know my love isn't enough to keep him safe or to bridge the gap that always threatens to form—that always *will* form—between two people. It isn't enough to save us from what I can't imagine. Scott was loved.

And though in general *understanding* is a lost cause, there have been moments when information felt helpful. One of those moments was inside the office of a Harvard psychotherapist named Stan Wiman.

I made an appointment with Stan because *psychotic break* was still the only language I'd heard to describe what happened to Scott, and it still didn't sound real to me. I wanted to understand it. I wanted to know if someone could, as it sometimes seemed Scott had, murder someone and then go back to normal afterward. Or was he not normal at all? Would he never be again?

On a gray afternoon in winter, I walked through the Harvard campus and through Harvard Square, past the old Au Bon Pain where I used to go every Wednesday afternoon with my mother. Back then, we'd order raspberry cheese croissants and Oranginas and sit outside to watch the men play chess while the pigeons hunted under their feet for crumbs. There were no chess tables there anymore.

I took the elevator to the fourth floor of the Holyoke Center, which was always under construction, and as I sat in the waiting room, I felt a fluttery nervousness and told myself there was no reason for it. When Stan came to get me, the first thing I noticed about him was his light blue eyes. He was slight, wearing a brown corduroy jacket. He welcomed me down the hall and into his office, where a fat

DSM-IV (the *Diagnostic and Statistical Manual of Mental Disorders*, the enormous tome of diagnoses published by the American Psychiatric Association that the law relies on) rested on the edge of his desk, as if it had just been used, which I took as a good sign. This is a person grounded in science, I thought.

Stan asked me why I made the appointment to see him, and I stumbled through the story of Scott, trying to articulate my desire to understand what had happened to him. He nodded along the way, making small sounds of sympathy and wincing where appropriate. I tried to make it clear that I was not there to talk about myself or my feelings, but was seeking something practical: an answer to the question of diagnosis.

I want to understand what a psychotic break is, I said, *and if it's . . . a real medical event. A real diagnosis.*

Stan blinked and nodded. *Psychosis*, he said, *is real. And really, a psychotic break is just intense fear.*

He went on: *It's a defense against fear or intense pressure. Do you have a sense of what your cousin might have felt afraid of? Anything he might have needed to defend himself against?*

I thought for a second. *No*, I said, *I don't really know, I didn't know him well.*

Then he asked me questions about myself and about my dreams. I told him about the recurring dream of the baby I was supposed to take care of but couldn't find, which I'd kept having. He asked me if I thought the baby was Scott. Then he asked if it was Ryan, the boy Scott killed. I said I didn't know.

As I walked home from Stan's office, it started to snow big fat flakes like cotton. And then the wind picked up, and as I stuffed my hands in my pockets to find my mittens, I realized one had fallen out, so I walked quickly to make myself warmer but I felt only cold.

I was struck by the idea of psychosis as defense. At home that night, alone, I looked up defense mechanisms. The internet led me to Freud, who wrote that defense mechanisms occur when our ego cannot meet the demands of reality. Often, he suggests, we end up defending ourselves against our own insupportable impulses. His oldest daughter, Anna Freud, elaborated on this research in *The Ego and the Mechanisms of Defense*, in which she outlined seven main tactics human beings deploy when anxiety becomes intolerable. Tactics like *repression*, *projection*, and *turning against the self*. We all defend ourselves—it's how we do so that matters. This is why the *DSM-IV* breaks the list of defense mechanisms into levels of maturity.* Can you find yourself in the list?

---

* Our modern understanding of defense mechanisms, as reflected in the *DSM-IV*, relies on the scholarship of George Eman Vaillant more than anyone else. Vaillant was a Harvard doctor made famous by his longtime happiness study, the major finding of which has proven, over the decades, to be the importance of relationships and the deadliness of loneliness.

Defense Levels and Individual Defense Mechanisms

High adaptive level. This level of defensive functioning results in optimal adaptation in the handling of stressors. These defenses usually maximize gratification and allow the conscious awareness of feelings, ideas, and their consequences. They also promote an optimum balance among conflicting motives. Examples of defenses at this level are

- anticipation
- affiliation
- altruism
- humor
- self-assertion
- self-observation
- sublimation
- suppression

Mental inhibitions (compromise formation) level. Defensive functioning at this level keeps potentially threatening ideas, feelings, memories, wishes, or fears out of awareness. Examples are

- displacement
- dissociation
- intellectualization
- isolation of affect
- reaction formation
- repression
- undoing

Minor image-distorting level. This level is characterized by distortions in the image of the self, body, or others that may be employed to regulate self-esteem. Examples are

- devaluation
- idealization
- omnipotence

Disavowal level. This level is characterized by keeping unpleasant or unacceptable stressors, impulses, ideas, affects, or responsibility out of awareness with or without a misattribution of these to external causes. Examples are

- denial
- projection
- rationalization

Major image-distorting level. This level is characterized by gross distortion or misattribution of the image of self or others. Examples are

- autistic fantasy
- projective identification
- splitting of self-image or image of others

Action level. This level is characterized by defensive functioning that deals with internal or external stressors by action or withdrawal. Examples are

- acting out
- apathetic withdrawal

- help-rejecting
  complaining
- passive
  aggression

Level of defensive dysregulation. This level is characterized by failure of defensive regulation to contain the individual's reaction to stressors, leading to a pronounced break with objective reality. Examples are

- delusional
  projection
- psychotic
  distortion
- psychotic denial

When I read about *turning against the self*, I think of a woman I know, a friend of a friend, who adopted a little boy from China. She and her husband had three children before they chose to adopt, so they had a sense, they thought, of what lay ahead. Their adopted son, Yu'Wen, had been abandoned in a field when he was ten months old. After being found, he spent three years in an orphanage, where he was diagnosed with cerebral palsy. Shortly after this, my friend's friend took him home to Virginia. Although he was three years old by this point, she held him that first night like a baby and he fell asleep in her arms.

But over the following weeks and months, my friend's friend said the boy started trying to make himself unlovable. He screamed at his new parents, and told anyone who would listen, out in public, at first in Chinese and then in English, that he wasn't being fed enough, that he didn't want to take a bath (*help-rejecting complaining*). When he got upset, he scratched his own skin and pounded his legs with his fists (*turning against the self*). One night, just before falling asleep, he told his new mother that he wanted to go back to China. *In case you decide not to keep me*, he said.

In case. The possibility of loss so certain in his short life.

How much are you willing to lose to keep yourself from loss? A family? A fluorescent squid arm? At the level of instinct, willingness has nothing to do with it. Animals sacrifice their bodies and blood because the stakes are life or death.

Humans often act as if we're skirting death even though we rarely are, in a literal sense. Yu'Wen's defenses are more rational than most—left to die in a field, he learned right away that survival is a question. But for most of us, our instincts for self-preservation have come unhinged from real-life threat. We experience fear in our animal bodies as we used to when we were fighting for our lives in prehistoric forests, but now we are defending ourselves against our own minds, against fear itself. Fear of future loss. Fear of our own instincts—instincts for violence, comfort, sex. Fear and hatred of the shame that these instincts inspire.

In *Violence*, James Gilligan observes that most violence starts in shame and grasps at desperate self-preservation:

> *The assertion that men do not kill for no reason is often truer the more "unprovoked" the killing appears to be. A man only kills another when he is, as he sees it, fighting to save himself, his own self— when he feels he is in danger of experiencing . . . the "death of the self," unless he engages in violence.*

A choice that feels like life or death is not really a choice, even if the danger is delusional.

AFTER MY APPOINTMENT WITH THE HARVARD PSYCHO-therapist the Supreme Court handed down its decision in *Montgomery v. Louisiana*,* the fourth in a series of cases about teenagers who break the law, following *Roper*, *Graham*, and *Miller*. In *Montgomery*, you could say the question was technical. It asked whether *Miller* should apply retroactively. And the Court ruled 6–3 that it should. This meant that all the people who were serving LWOP sentences for crimes they committed when they were teenagers before *Miller*, no matter how long ago, needed to be resentenced or offered parole hearings. If it was a technical ques-

---

* *Montgomery v. Louisiana*, 136 S. Ct. 718 (2016).

tion before the Court, the application of its answer was alive and beating. The *Montgomery* decision meant hope and a chance for freedom for hundreds who'd been without either.

The decision also doubled down on *Miller*'s dicta about rareness. In his majority opinion, Justice Kennedy wrote:

> *Although* Miller *did not foreclose a sentencer's ability to impose life without parole on a juvenile, the* Court *explained that a lifetime in prison is a disproportionate sentence for all but the rarest of children, those whose crimes reflect "irreparable corruption."*

Like the others before it, *Montgomery* felt like part of a shift. When I spoke with Scott on the phone that week and I started to talk excitedly about the case, he was quiet. I heard in his quiet a signal to back off. Then he said, *Even if the law changed, it would always carve out an exception for me.* At first I protested but quickly lost confidence.

Later I went back to the text of the decisions. There *was* momentum in the quartet formed by *Roper*, *Graham*, *Miller*, and *Montgomery*, which suggested we might be moving toward something new. But Scott was right that each case preserved the idea of *permanent incorrigibility*. Or, as Justice Kennedy calls it in *Montgomery*, *irreparable corruption*. The exception, the carve-out.

But how could judges know whether a teenager's incorrigibility is permanent? Whether what's broken is irreparable? Legally, *irreparable corruption* is a subjective standard that considers character, background, and the full circumstances around a crime. It also requires the sentencer to forecast into the future, to make a prediction about the likelihood of change for the better.

Here's a story about who we have decided is capable of making such a determination. The petitioner before the Court in *Montgomery* was a man named Henry Montgomery. Montgomery, who is Black, shot and killed a white police officer in East Baton Rouge Parish in 1963. He was seventeen at the time of the crime. A jury originally sentenced him to be executed, but in 1966, he appealed, and the court reversed that sentence due to "community prejudice." The Ku Klux Klan had affected the climate of the original trial. Montgomery was sentenced to life without parole at Angola. When he appealed his sentence based on *Miller*, he had spent fifty years there. During that time, he'd started a boxing club to help inmates learn self-defense and discipline and find community, and he'd garnered only twenty-three write-ups, impressively few for so many years. The most recent write-ups related to smoking a cigarette and having his laundry on top of a locker. This did not seem like a man of irreparable corruption.

But as of this writing, three years after the Supreme Court

remanded his sentence and issued a mandate in his name, Henry Montgomery, now in his seventies, is still serving his life sentence at Angola. He's been denied parole on two separate occasions since his Supreme Court victory. The last parole hearing took place in April 2019. Three people sat on the parole board. Two of them voted in favor of parole, but the decision must be unanimous. The board member who voted against him is a physical therapist named Brennan Kelsey, appointed to the board by Governor John Bel Edwards. Kelsey and Edwards have been friends for years. When Kelsey announced his decision to deny parole, he cited as his reason Montgomery's lack of participation in enough programs while in prison. "I think that's a lack of maturity," he said. "It's your responsibility to continue to work hard on the inside. . . . Take as many programs as you can. Continue to work hard. But that's my vote for today."

There is something unspeakable about this scene. A white man in his forties or fifties, telling a Black man in his seventies—who committed a crime over fifty years ago, who was sentenced to die by a jury that the Ku Klux Klan influenced—to work harder. Montgomery had won at the Supreme Court, but he is still sentenced to die at Angola. When his lawyer told him the board's decision, reporters describe his face flashing with neither anger nor sadness but confusion. It didn't make any sense. It didn't make moral sense. A legal decree without moral sense—i.e., without justice—is an act of violence.* Is it evil?

AT FIRST, WHEN SCOTT MURDERED RYAN, I WAS FELLED by the moral ambiguity. Had my sixteen-year-old cousin committed an evil act? Or a sick act? Should he be shown mercy through treatment, or retribution through our legal system? The murder revealed a world in which chaos reigned. I needed something to hold on to. I wanted to build a house of belief that the floods could not wash away. I looked outward. I got back to law school and saw Bryan Stevenson speak and learned about juvenile justice and taught inside carceral institutions and worked on lawsuits against these institutions. I started gathering stones of certainty. In building, I was interested in fortitude, not nuance. I wanted to build something impervious to acts of God. My beliefs grew solid and tall, like walls. If you'd asked me then, in those years, I would have told you to open all the prisons, to let everyone go, to burn the system down. Jesus said:

> *The Spirit of the Lord is on me, because he has*
> *anointed me to proclaim good news to the poor. He*

---

* In some ways, all legal decrees and decisions are acts of violence. From Robert M. Cover's "Violence and the Word": "Legal interpretive acts signal and occasion the imposition of violence upon others. . . . Between the idea and the reality of common meaning falls the shadow of the violence of law, itself."

has sent me to proclaim freedom for the prisoners and
recovery of sight for the blind, to set the oppressed
free, to proclaim the year of the Lord's favor.

I believed in freedom for the prisoners. I still do.

But after I left D.C. and got married, started writing and started a family, I felt certainty diminish. It was one thing to shout *Freedom for the prisoners*, another to proclaim it in the particular. Did Scott deserve freedom? Was I discounting the pain of Ryan's family, who wants Scott in prison, and of all victims who say they feel safer and more satisfied by longer sentences? What kind of systemic change is possible and what will work to make it real? Riots seem more effective than nonprofits, but theoretically, I believed in peace. I stepped back from my lofty ideals. And at first this growing uncertainty made me quiet. But then I figured out that uncertainty wasn't only an absence, empty air and space, but a thing with its own shape and texture. My mother says, *In poetry, the answers are in the language.* She also says, *In life, the solution is in the problem.* I needed to push language into these questions like light. Through writing, I see how this is a story about losing, finding, losing again, and searching for certainty.

I AM DOWSING FOR MERCY LIKE WATER BELOW THE dirt of these words. I'm interested in a mercy that's *particular*. My previous certainty expressed a blanket mercy, political mercy. *Freedom for the prisoners.* I don't think that's wrong, but I want to get there the hard way—after grappling with the details. What does mercy look like when the details scramble your instincts for sympathy? When there's no mitigation? When there's no easy answer to the question *why?*

On appeal, the circuit court said about Scott's case: *There is no mitigation.* What they meant is that there was no abuse or poverty, there was no disadvantage or neglect, there was not even a legal diagnosis. This was an upper-middle-class white teenager who walked out one day and killed a child.

What does mercy look like when a crime's brutality makes your stomach turn? The near decapitation of a nine-year-old boy, riding bikes with his mother, and the theorizing about doing it again, to a woman, afterward. The mass murder of more than twenty children and teachers. The terrorist, racist slaughter of nine Black congregants in prayer. These crimes defy my natural capacity for empathy. Toward the end of her profile on Dylann Roof, Ghansah writes, *I know that he is hatred.* Is Scott *hatred*, too? Is hatred what I mean when I say evil?

In Scott, I see a self-hatred turned outward. *When an inner situation is not made conscious, it happens outside as fate.* It's hard not to pathologize hatred and violent crime. You could understand everything in terms of illness. You could let undiagnosed illness do the work of explanation, which opens the door for at least pity, a possible precursor to empathy and mercy.

But I mistrust this convenience. About Roof's violence, Bryan Stevenson says in an interview:

> [A] young white man going into a historic black church and slaughtering people in this way couldn't be understood outside the context of our racial history of violence and terror directed at black people. And so, my thoughts about our failure to deal more effectively with that history were also right on the surface.... The question I ask is not how could this young man be affected by these historic failures, by this ideology, the question is how could he not? We're all affected by it.

How could he not? is a question infused with mercy. It is a much harder road to follow. Both Ghansah and Stevenson are doing more than pathologizing. They're widening the scope of the lens. All efforts of understanding are acts of mercy.

JUST BEFORE THE SOLAR ECLIPSE, I TAKE A PREGNANCY test and watch two lines emerge like pink ghosts. We are living in Vermont in my parents' house while we look for a place to live on our own. This is itself a kind of miracle, or at least proof that things can change (which might be a working definition of *miracle*, at least in terms of families and systems). That my parents would have us stay, that we would want to—all of us having survived one another's drinking and fighting and then the slow work of recovery, delivering us into some new version of togetherness.

On the day of the eclipse, I drive down the dirt road to the public library in the village, where they have saved twenty pairs of special eclipse-watching glasses. I want to stare directly at the sun. My father meets me there. Sitting on a blanket in front of the library, I say, *I have something to tell you*, but he knows right away what I'm going to say, so I don't have to say anything else. He's so happy that he calls me Katie by accident, and we laugh because he's never called me that before. He says, *We're going to take good care of you.*

I used to be afraid of my father. He was rageful and his drinking fueled his rage like gasoline on fire. Time with him felt like the earth was always about to open up. But over the years and before my eyes, he tried to change and did change. He told me his own *why*, pointing back at his childhood. He called himself a survivor, a slow learner. *I was doing my best*, he said.

This looking back was important. I tried to understand his story, and did understand it in pieces, in a logical sense, but my fear—which looked a lot like anger at some points—

didn't dissipate until the change in him lasted. This hurt his feelings. It felt like I was holding him to an unfair standard, and maybe I was. But I couldn't settle into loving him clearly, without anger, until he settled down enough to let me settle, too. Until it felt safe. Without the smoke and fire, I could see him clearly, and what was there was love.

What I'm saying is: understanding is the work of mercy. But it doesn't deliver forgiveness or real healing—at least it didn't for me—until there is something else, too, and perhaps this thing is best called Time. Time for things to shift and open, for smoke to clear. Some combination of *Chronos*, which is quantitative, and *Kairos*, which is qualitative, lasting. Years plus grace. Hours plus mercy. I don't think all cracks heal, but between me and my father, what was broken eventually let love in.

In the shadow of the moon, the light from the eclipse was more than the absence of sun. It was cool and supernatural, casting us in new light.

THAT SAME WEEK, SCOTT'S MOTHER CALLS TO TELL ME I've been added to the prison's list of approved visitors, and I book a flight to Louisiana to see him for the first time since before the murder. A few days later, my mother gets a call from her doctor with a cancer diagnosis. Her prognosis is good, they say, but she'll need an operation and maybe radiation. She cries quietly after the call, and I lie next to her on the floor, not saying much except for *You're going to be okay*. But she and I both know I don't know that. When I was little, she always used to say, *Any damn thing can happen*. It's hard to find comfort in uncertainty, the expectation of chaos. Others look harder for the patterns—

> *If cancer strikes you*
> *as random or chaotic,*
>
> *remember that like*
> *every other algorithm,*
>
> *it too has a unique function,*
> *the elegance of its own logic.*

Where can I find the algorithm for loss, and if I find it would its elegance help me survive?

FEAR OF LOSING CAME QUICKLY ON THE HEELS OF knowing I was pregnant. For four days after the test, I was happy. On day five, the idea of loss set up its empty shop. One morning I woke up certain I'd lost him. I opened my eyes in bed and felt mourning coursing through my body, and cramps, and I *knew*. But I was wrong—despite the fear, he kept on growing. Fear can feel so much like knowing. My job, it became clear quickly, was to beat back fear, which I found I could achieve only through surrender.

I dove headlong into Buddhism during my pregnancy, because letting go was the antithesis of even the earliest parental instincts. I thought often of the story of Milarepa, who returns to his home one day to find it filled with demons. They wouldn't go away until he invited them to stay. Once they were invited in, they disappeared, except for the last, most fearsome demon, who wouldn't leave. So Milarepa walked straight into the demon's mouth, daring it to chomp down, at which point it vanished. I tried to surrender to the fear of loss like that. I wanted to walk inside its mouth. The solution is inside the problem.

Still, I left every uneventful ultrasound feeling like we'd had a lucky break. At the twenty-week scan, the medical technician examined the baby's anatomy in detail, measuring and counting, silently recording without comment. On the screen, I saw *HIGH RISK*. I didn't know why, and then I remembered my brother.

When I was five years old, my parents discovered that the baby growing inside my mother would be born without a left forearm and hand. I sat in a chair against the wall of the small, dark ultrasound room when the doctor told my parents about the anomaly. She told them that they were well within the safe range for an abortion, which made my mother start to cry, which made me want to cry, too. I stood up and walked to my father, who was standing by her side, and wrapped my arm around his knees and felt my cheek against his jeans.

But the truth is that I didn't understand why they were so sad. I assumed I'd missed something the doctor said, something very serious. In the car on the way home, I asked them from the back seat if the baby was going to live, and they said, *Oh, honey, of course*, and I said, *So what's the big deal?* I couldn't fathom the news to be a loss, as it was for them, who already knew the world to be something to survive, and who believed that disability was disadvantage. In the ultrasound room, they lost what they'd assumed their son would have: the same chances as everyone else at happiness and survival.

Years later, my father tells me that in that moment he felt betrayed. *I'd been good*, he says. *I'd cleaned up my act*, by which he means he'd stopped snorting coke and smoking cigarettes and gotten married and moved to the suburbs. But it was like it hadn't mattered, he says. All bets were off. *If this could happen, anything could happen. What would happen next? What would God let happen next?*

My father was keeping up his end of a contract—*I was good, I'd cleaned up my act*—but it was a contract *void ab initio* (invalid at the outset). The contract is void because there's no law to enforce it, no signatory on the other side.

MY BEST FRIEND FROM LAW SCHOOL HAD A BABY WHOSE heart was constantly threatening to get too strong.

He was her third child, her first boy. There was no warning, no signs during ultrasounds. When he was in her arms on the late night of his birth, the nurses heard an abnormal heartbeat, a murmur, but no one was worried. Holes in the heart are common at birth. Usually they're small and close up on their own. They call this a *murmur* because when there's a hole in your heart it makes a sound like a whooshing, which is the sound of turbulent blood, like a whispering. No one was worried.

But then the next morning, the cardiologist came in and the air in the room changed. The new story rolled out slowly at first and then quickly. My friend's first unsaid thought she calls selfish: *I can't believe this is happening to me.* I tell her everyone thinks this when the story changes.

After a few tests, they learned that the problem was the aortic valve. Her son's was deformed, dysplastic, with only one leaflet instead of three, which inhibits blood flow, which causes the heart to work triply hard to pump blood. When it has to work so hard to pump blood, the muscles of the heart walls strengthen until they are too thick to function, which can cause the heart to fail.

Through the first six days, the outlook got worse and worse. Two-month hospital stay, uncertain odds. Open-heart surgery on a heart so small is precarious. My friend was full of logistical questions that the surgeons couldn't answer. Breast milk and pumping schedules. Visiting with her other two toddlers during an extended ICU stay. The women working at the hospital, the social workers and nurses, were more helpful. She called me weeping from a hallway. After crying, she sounded empty, almost numb. *Is this grief?* she wondered. *I think I'm in shock*, she told me.

But then a less invasive procedure was advanced and scheduled. A valvuloplasty, where they go in through the groin with a catheter and stretch the valve with a balloon. She had two weeks to get her baby as strong as possible before the operation. She nursed him through the day and night. Creases started to form at his wrists and thighs, the signs of fatness she wanted to see. His cheeks got puffy. *Prosperous*, we joked.

Before the procedure, the doctor told her to pack a bag for a week, in case they needed to stay. But after it was done, the surgeons came out smiling. *We feel good*, they said. *What does that mean?* my friend asked. *What's next?* The surgeons laughed. Their job was done for the day.

Before the surgery, the doctors said, *We are going to consider this a huge success if this buys us a year before another intervention.* At this, my friend was incredulous, despondent. She couldn't imagine having to go through another surgery only a year from then. But now, more than a year later, she gets it. *Time has changed*, she says. Every extra week is good. *So much of this*, she says, *is getting used to not knowing what's next, living with uncertainty.*

She has walked through a door into life's fragility and now she can never unknow it. *Is that heartbreak?* I ask her. She says she doesn't know—she's unable to feel her own heart. She is wrapped around her son's, a heart and heartbeat that's been absorbed into her own body under the spell of vigilance. *Listen, / how your heart pounds inside me,* writes the poet Wisława Szymborska in her poem "Could Have."

God willing, she says, *he will have a good and long life, but he'll always know his cardiologist. He'll have monthly appointments to listen to his heartbeat. He won't play sports.*

You could say his heart is broken. And like other kinds of heartbreak, he'll likely never be without it. Neuroscientists say that love and heartbreak are not feelings but physiological states. Emotions come and go like weather. But a *state* doesn't disappear on a good day. You can move across the country and it goes with you. You can get married and have children, it will stay. You learn to live with it, form around it like water over rock.

NOTHING IS TOO SACRED OR BELOVED NOT TO FALL apart. When you learn this in your life, the answer to the question *why* becomes *why not?* For my father, it was Sam's ultrasound. For my law school friend, her son's heart. Scott's crime smashed home the lesson for me. Not only did I lose faith in the justice system I was learning about, but I also lost faith in *life*, my own and the whole project generally. Every good day felt like luck. Every safe drive, every routine ultrasound. Luck can run out on any normal blue-sky Thursday.

But in truth, if Scott's crime is what brought it home, it was a lesson I'd been learning long before that day in June. Waiting for the other shoe to drop was a game I'd learned from my parents, who'd learned it themselves inside the burned-down houses and abuse and murders and heart-break of their own lives. In a recent short story in *The New Yorker*, Lauren Groff describes inherited trauma as "a silent wind." The narrator says, of her mother:

> *She tried her best, but she couldn't help filling me with this same wind. It seeped into me through her blood. . . . She was far from being the first to find it blowing through her, and of course I will not be the last. I look around and can see it in so many other women, passed down from a time beyond history, this wind that is dark and ceaseless and raging within.*

RETURNING TO THE ROOTS—

The Indo-European root of the word *heart* is *kerd* (think cardia, cordate), which may come from *kred-dhǝ*, which means *to place trust in*. And *break* derives from the Old English *brecan*, the Indo-European root of which is *bhreg*. *Bhreg* has many associations across languages—in old French, *brier*, a dialectal variant of *broyer*, which means *to knead*, and in old Norse, *brakni*, which means *undergrowth*. A rupture in the trust you put in life or love. Being kneaded, broken down. The path interrupted by a thicket. The solution lives in the language: being kneaded is also to be prepared. In one sense the thickets interrupt the path, and in another sense they're a part of the path itself.

THE DAY BEFORE I LEAVE FOR LOUISIANA TO VISIT
Scott at Angola, our midwife comes to the house and has
me lie down on the couch in my parents' living room. I roll
up my shirt and she squirts some gel on my stomach, which
is only slightly swollen, and uses a doppler to search for
the heartbeat. She warns us that if we don't hear it today, it
doesn't mean anything is wrong. It's still early, and sometimes it's hard to find it with her old machine. I steel myself for silence. But she finds him. L is there, and we hold
hands and listen to the rhythm. It sounds like something
otherworldly, a great discovery, evidence of life on Mars,
but also *home*. Listening to his heart, I imagine him listening to mine, twin drums.

Some things you don't forget. I will never forget hearing
my son's heartbeat for the first time, and I will never forget driving to Angola Prison early on a Saturday morning
in October. Perhaps due to their proximity in time, these
moments have fused together in my memory, so that as I
remember one, I remember the other. Sometimes there is
early-morning fog in my memory of the heartbeat. Sometimes there is a heartbeat, like a bird's beating wings, carrying me along the road to the prison.

From West Feliciana, the way to Angola is easy to nav-
igate: Route 61 to 66, which takes you in the whole way.
Slowly the strip malls give way to trailer homes, which give

way to farms. I set out early, hoping to catch one of the first buses from the prison's front gates, so the mist sitting low in the fields catches the light of the sun as it rises. It all has the texture of a dream.

I try to regulate my nerves by taking slow, deep breaths.

I pull through the gates of the prison and park the car. A man is sitting in a parked car next to mine. He signals for me to roll down my window, which I do, and he asks if I have an extra pair of pants. He'd driven all night to visit his son, and now can't get into the prison because he's wearing shorts. I told him I didn't. *I'm so sorry*, I say.

Through the front doors, the first thing you see is a metal detector and a conveyor belt where you have to put all your things, like airport security. The guards send me back to the car three times to return contraband—my cell phone, notebook, ChapStick. These rules I curse as I run through the parking lot for a fourth time, not wanting to miss the first bus. These regulations and codes, jamming us up. A man who has driven all night to see his son won't be able to because of the length of his pants.

Before finally stepping through the metal detector, I ask a guard if it matters that I'm pregnant. I whispered it like a secret. *This won't hurt you*, she says, but something in the way she says it and waves me through makes me unsure that she knows or cares one way or another.

Though it's just past eight a.m., the waiting room is

filling up. Pieces of families, mostly Black, more women than men. Some people greet one another with a nod or good morning, but overall we seem to avoid eye contact, despite, or maybe because of, the thing we have in common—the incarceration of someone important enough to visit on a Saturday morning. In this case, shared experience doesn't translate readily to fellowship. Maybe that's the work of separation that shame undertakes. We wait inside our private stories like boats at sea.

Finally, two buses come, and a freeman—that's what they call guards at Angola, "freemen"—reads out the names of prisoners from a clipboard.

Scott McCabe, he says, and I stand and walk through the waiting-room doors out into the sun, where there are two blue buses idling in the circular driveway. I board the bus that the freeman points to and pick a seat somewhere in the middle, which makes me feel suddenly very young, like a child on a field trip with no friends. As we pull away, I watch the blue sky over the green fields out the window, fields marked by pretty white fences. Stop sign intersections decorated with manicured shrubs and autumnal displays of pumpkins, gourds, corncobs, and mums. I don't understand it; it looks like a town from a Lifetime movie about rekindled romance, diners, and drive-ins.

I'd imagined a grimmer scene not just because Angola is a prison but because for decades it was called *America's bloodiest prison*. When Scott was sentenced here, his defense attorney was afraid Scott might not make it through his first night. That was how pervasive violence and sexual assault seemed to be from the outside—a perception based on decades of stories and reports.

In 1951, thirty-one inmates sliced their Achilles tendons with razor blades in protest of the conditions. The inhumane cells, the unconscionable hours of work in the fields, the lack of medical care. In the early seventies, an average of twelve prisoners were stabbed to death each year. Though the annual loss of life has lessened today and conditions have somewhat improved, the state penitentiary still shines as an example of our ignominious system. It's the biggest maximum-security prison in the country, with 6,300 prisoners and 1,800 staff members.

Eighty-five percent of those prisoners are serving life sentences.

The average sentence for non-lifers is eighty-nine years.

That means that Louisiana boasts the highest number of people in prison per capita in the country, and because the United States leads the world in prisoners per capita, Louisiana takes the world title.

The state benefits from this superlative status through an archaic system of work release, which allows a qualified prisoner to work, for instance, at the governor's mansion as a butler, or washing cars at the police department, while almost all of his paycheck feeds back to the state.

This work-release program hews closely to Angola's original incarnation as a plantation. In the early nineteenth century, a man named Francis Rout owned and operated the eight-thousand-acre plot for cotton, calling it Angola because that's where many of the enslaved people who worked there were from. In 1880, the Confederate major Samuel Lawrence James bought the land and continued to harvest its crops through a convict-lease system, whereby Major James "rented" convicts from the state. These convicts lived on the plantation and were treated brutally—underfed, physically abused, sometimes worked to literal death. But the state was making money, so the system stood until 1901, when reports started getting out about the brutality and the state was pressured to take it over as its own penitentiary.

Unsurprisingly, this did not improve conditions. For one thing, the state's interests in profit, in saving and making money, were at odds with the interests of the men living at Angola who could provide a force of unpaid labor, a work-around for slavery's inconvenient illegality. And for another, Angola has always been pitted against nature, unnatural in every way. The land is bound on three sides by the Mississippi River, which has meant frequent flooding and the degradation of living quarters and the ruin of crops, which used to be the prison's source of funding. When crops suffered in the early twentieth century, the prison didn't have the cash to fix broken toilets or heat cells or put in fans or tend to medical emergencies. As if in protest, Nature has seemed to push against Angola for what goes on there: a moral violation of the very earth on which it sits.

Today the prison stretches across eighteen thousand acres, a parcel bigger than the size of Manhattan. And because the prison still operates its crops, on any given day you will see men, mostly Black, doing field work.

Where am I? I think again as I ride the bus. When *am I? This is your country*, my mind whispers back to itself. I see a green sign outside the window that reads *Bird Sanctuary*. I think of the preserved plantations of the antebellum South, all grandeur and pride of place, untarnished to the naked eye because the blood is in the soil. Dissonance is one of America's chief traits.

My bus makes several stops at various "camps" along the way—low-slung buildings where prisoners live—emptying out a little more at each stop so that by the time we arrive at death row, where there are no more corncobs and mums, only two of us remain on the bus. Me and a skinny white man in a crumpled suit. I keep wondering about his family, about who he might be here to see—a brother, a son?—but he doesn't catch my eye.

As we walk along the chain-link fence, through two more checkpoints, I think about the other prisons I've been to, in Stockton, San Rafael, Baltimore. These experiences make the security rituals easier, but this day is different because

I'm not shielded by a job to do. This is my family. This is my first time seeing Scott since we were children.

Inside the lights are dim and my eyes take a second to adjust. A guard asks me and the skinny man to sign our names in a book, along with the time and date. It turns out the man is an attorney visiting a client and for some reason this makes me feel lonely, like he betrayed our shared journey—but it was never shared. Out of all the people in the crowded waiting room that morning, I'm the only one who made it this far from the gates. As if my own goodness or sin is implicated in how deep inside the prison I had to travel. *It happened, but not to you*, writes Szymborska.

Then the guard escorts me down a long hallway to the visitation room. It's nothing like the scene in *The Silence of the Lambs* when Jodie Foster has to walk down a row of cells separated only by bars. The walls here are solid concrete and I'd have to crane my neck to see anybody inside, which I don't. Still, as I sit at the table by myself waiting for Scott, I hear a voice inside my own head: *Am I safe?*

In the past, I dismissed the question on principle. When other people asked, *Do you feel safe teaching at the prison? Aren't you scared?* the inquiries felt barbed with assumptions I wanted to annihilate: Prisoners are bad, dangerous. Women are fragile. *Actually*, I would say, *prison is one of the safest places I could be. My students are some of the nicest men I know.*

But there was that story of the volunteer at a prison in—
Colorado? Arizona?—being stabbed with a pencil and
raped. The thought of that woman rises to the surface and
I push it away. The problem is: now my body is more than
mine to forget. I'm home to a quickening, a becoming—cells
dividing, heart chambers and toes taking shape—a life I
don't love yet but know it's my purpose to protect. What if
those people were right when they asked me if I was afraid,
what if Scott isn't as okay as I think, what if there's a prison
riot? Visitors to prisons are warned that if you are taken as
a hostage, or if there is a riot, guards will not save your life
over defending the gates.

And then, in the midst of these questions, Scott's face appears in the narrow window of the door. He smiles slightly,
shyly.

Another mother's son. At one point, before murder and
prison, a baby inside a body. Cells dividing, heart chambers
and toes taking shape. It's obvious, but in its private clarity
it has the force of a revelation. The heavy door unlocks, and
he walks in, pausing so that the guard behind him can undo
the handcuffs around his wrists. The shackles around his
ankles remain. I stand up—*Am I allowed to hug you?* I ask,
and he says, *Yes.*

THE NEXT DAY, I ATTEND THE ANGOLA PRISON RODEO
with my friend who's a journalist. She's visiting Louisiana

— 182 —

for a feature on the state's efforts at prison reform, given its long list of *most*s and *highest*s. When we found out we were going to be in Louisiana at the same time, we decided to share a hotel room. She's covering the rodeo for a shorter column in her paper.

Angola's is one of the only prison rodeos left in the country. Most have shut down for liability or profitability concerns. But despite ongoing efforts to end the tradition by prison reform activists who say it's inhumane, the Angola rodeo is in its fifty-third year when we arrive. It takes place once in the spring and every Sunday in October, selling out each weekend to as many as thirteen thousand attendees.

The scene is like other rural fairs, with a few dark twists that paint the day in something of the uncanny. There are booths with fried food, handmade goods like carved wooden boxes and leather belts sold at tables—but the men behind the tables are wearing prisoner uniforms. There's a merry-go-round and live music and a photo booth where you can have your picture taken "behind bars."

All the men participating in the fair and the rodeo itself are doing so because they choose to, but you don't have to bend over backward to question the very nature of *choice* inside a prison. Some men see it as a welcome distraction from the monotony of prison life, an opportunity to have a moment in the spotlight or make money (there are cash prizes for rodeo winners) or socialize outside the dorms. Others, including Scott, see it as exploitive. The big problem is that the rodeo is cruel in its spirit, a vestige of another time. So whether the men sign up themselves or not, the nature of the games—a series of gladiator-like events, unmatched by other standard rodeos throughout the South and West—strips them of humanity for sport.

We take our seats in the stadium. It's hard to hear in the bleachers. Families with little kids, groups of teenagers, women in jean cutoffs and cowboy boots on dates with men sporting prominent belts. The tamest events involve men riding an angry bull, like a normal rodeo. But things take a turn a little ways in. I look down at the program and see "inmate pinball." I point it out to my friend and she makes an "I don't know" face. When it begins, a half dozen men walk out and take their places standing in the center of Hula-Hoops scattered around the dusty ring. Then the goaded bull gets released into their midst. The challenge for the men is to stay put. Several are immediately flipped up into the air by the bull's horns or trampled under its hooves. An ambulance waits in the wings, just outside the arena. It's needed only once that day.

What's clear is that these bodies are disposable. The audience is mostly white, but the prisoners are mostly Black.

I tell my friend I can't watch anymore. It's too awful, too hot, and there's no wind and my morning sickness is back. We head down to the grassy area and get huge plastic cups of lemonade, loaded with ice and straight sugar. On our way out, as I drive through the Angola prison gates for the second time in two days, I feel how deeply I want to go home, how bad I want to get *out*. How lucky I am to leave.

A week later, after I'm back, a letter arrives from Scott. *Thank you for making my day*, he writes.

I COULD TELL YOU THIS STORY WHILE WALKING OUT OF THIS story, writes Maggie Nelson. That's what I wanted in the beginning, too. A way out. But seven years later, when I left Scott at the prison that Saturday afternoon after spending the day talking about books and eating French fries from the commissary, when I said goodbye and walked down the long, dark hallway away from him, his ankles in chains, and felt the tears on my cheeks, I realized that what I wanted most of all was for *him* to walk out.

I have longed for a second chance for Scott.

I have felt this desire in my heart more than my brain. Some days I trust it, believe its logic, and other days I don't. It emanates partly from the ties of blood, which are stronger than I knew. Being with Scott felt like being with family—an unexplainable familiarity, a current pulling me in.

But also my desire for a second chance comes from Jesus's instruction to *free the prisoners*, which I now understand in both its literal and metaphorical senses. I'd forgotten that

Jesus spoke mostly in metaphor. No matter what he said, he was always speaking about love—love and mercy.

THESE ARE BRYAN STEVENSON'S SUBJECTS, TOO, WHEN he writes in his book: *We are all broken by something. We have all hurt someone and have been hurt. We all share the condition of brokenness even if our brokenness is not equivalent.*

It is merciful to acknowledge what we share. But also to see clearly that the heartbreak of listening to the news is not equivalent to the heartbreak of a murdered or murdering child. Parents who survive that are on an island known to only those who land there through experience, that midnight boat of loss. And if our brokenness is not equivalent, neither is our healing. A few days after Creigh Deeds's son, Gus, attacked him and then shot himself, Deeds released a statement: *I am alive so must live. Some wounds won't heal.* Just as the wounds that Scott rendered won't heal. Not for Ryan's mother and father, brother and grandparents, who have had to go on without him. Nor for Scott himself, or the circle of people who love him. No law or judge or sentence, defense or restitution, could ever make them whole again. Not every heart will mend. "To Bhain Campbell," by John Berryman:

> I told a lie once in a verse. I said
> I said I said I said "The heart will mend,

Body will break and mend, the foam replace
For even the unconsolable his taken friend."
This is a lie. I had not been here then.

And yet
       And yet
              And yet against this certainty of broken-
ness, and the failures of healing, hope is possible.

I have learned to find it in *making*, in people making
beauty with their hands and brains and bodies—art, families, food, new laws. New laws that have their roots in justice and offer shade to the many rather than the few. Hala
Alyan writes in her poem "Spoiler":

I'm here to tell you the tide will never stop coming in.
I'm here to tell you whatever you build will be ruined,
so make it beautiful.

And then there is theology. Our oldest stories of wisdom
do not gloss over suffering but suggest a timeline that expands beyond what we can see, which allows for possibility.
I may not see the healing I crave in my lifetime, but that
means little for what healing is possible. Faith asks me to
believe in what I can only barely imagine. It is a theology
of possibility.

And if you were to translate this theology of possibility
to the law, you arrive at Bryan Stevenson's oral arguments in

front of the Supreme Court: *to say to any child that* you are fit only to die in prison *is cruel and unusual punishment*. The fact of possibility reduces life sentences for children to a profound immorality. Which, in turn, obviates *irreparable corruption*, an idea that's evidently impossible to divine with accuracy, since it so clearly does not describe most of the people to whom it's been applied—for instance, Henry Montgomery, Evan Miller, Kuntrell Jackson.

Nor does it describe Scott, who, over the years, I have watched put together a life. At first all he could do was read. He read nine hours a day. Then, he pushed and pushed to be able to take his GED, a years-long battle with the prison, and eventually they let him. Now he teaches Bible Study and takes victim awareness classes. His favorite book is currently Lauren Groff's short story collection *Florida*, which he asked me to send him twice, because he had to give it away when he was moved off death row but loved it enough to want to own it. He also loves Dante and comic books.

I don't know all the darkness he's moved through. I know there were times when he wanted to die. This was the desire he expressed when he killed a boy. But over time, he has built something in prison. This building and making will never change what he did, but it seems to me the opposite of irreparable—this putting together, this building after everything is broken.

SIFTING THROUGH WHAT'S COMPLICATED, I HAVE TRIED to find the kernel of what isn't. Something unassailable. This is what I have: Scott was a child when he took another child's life, and to say to him, *You are irredeemable and irreparable*, to make him die in prison without treatment, is a condemnation of possibility, which is a condemnation of ourselves. The carve-out preserved by the Supreme Court for *irreparable corruption* may be fair in certain cases, but it isn't just. Because where fairness measures, justice transforms. Its instrument is mercy.

ON AN ICY ROAD IN THE MIDDLE OF WINTER UNDER A pale blue sky I am clutching the steering wheel and asking for mercy. I am six months pregnant. I'm in the car because I'm going to find L, who just texted me: *Call 911. Accident on road. I'm in water.*

I'm at home when the text comes, and I want to call him but instead I grab the landline and dial 911. The operator is calm and says responders are on their way. When we hang up, I try calling L's phone but it goes straight to voicemail. I stand frozen in the kitchen, not knowing whether to stay at home so that 911 can call me back—isn't that something I read about crises? to stay where you are?—or get in the car to find him. I decide to find him. I know there are things I should bring with me, but I can't think what any of them are. I grab a blanket and run outside to the car.

The morning is clear and the winter looks harmless as it shimmers, but the roads are bad—dirt slick with ice from the frozen night. As I drive down the steepest hill, I start saying the Jesus prayer out loud to steady myself. *Lord Jesus Christ have mercy on me Lord Jesus Christ have mercy on me.* Then I drop it and just start saying *please.* I mean: *Please let me make it down this hill, please let L be okay, please let no one be killed.*

At the bottom of the hill, I round the bend to the left where the road meets the brook and a fire engine comes into view. Two other cars are there, too, but not ours. *I'm the wife*, I say inanely to a firefighter, after I park—and then I see him, sitting on the ground with a crinkly metal blanket around his shoulders, two EMTs talking to him, one, the woman, crouching down at his level. He stands up when he sees me and we hug. *I'm okay*, he says. *I love you*, he says. *I wanted to tell you that.* He's shaking. *I love you, too*, I say, and I wrap the blanket from the car around him. *What happened?* I say, and he tells me he tried to move over for another car coming toward him on the narrow road but his wheels slipped off into a snowbank and he couldn't get traction. The car skidded over the edge of the embankment, into the only deep part of the stream that winds along the road, at the mouth of the culvert. The car flipped upside down as it fell, crashing through the ice. Then it started to sink. In the car, he undid the seat belt and climbed right side up and tried to call for help but his phone wasn't working. That was when he texted me. He tried to get out, open the doors, but the ice he'd crashed into had the doors pinned shut. The car was filling with water. A neighbor driving on the road didn't see it happen, but she saw his absence—the car she'd just passed suddenly vanished in her rearview mirror—so she stopped, went back to check. She called her husband and father, who got L out of the car by breaking the ice with their boots. Then all three men swam out of the frozen water to land.

We need to get you out of these clothes, one of the paramedics says. *Do you have clothes for him?* a firefighter says, turning to me. No, I say, *but I can go get some, we live right up the road*. Why didn't I bring clothes? I think. They take L into the ambulance to strip him down. They're worried about hypothermia, they tell me, and they need to check him for injury.

On my way back to get clothes, I walk to the edge of the road and see our car upside down in the frozen water. It's completely submerged—all you can see is the undercarriage and wheels and I get it then, it hits me. *Yeah*, says one of the firefighters, looking at my face. *It's a miracle he's okay.*

This is something we hear again and again in the week afterward. The police officer who writes the report (*he's a lucky man*), the tow truck man (*he should be dead*), the insurance agent we talk to thirty times on the phone (*some-one was looking out for him that day*). A lucky break. L didn't feel lucky, but there are at least two versions to every story like this. One is about being unlucky (the ice, the snowdrift, being trapped in a car filling with water) and one is about being spared (the neighbor, the text, the moment L heard someone's voice shouting through the water and ice and he knew he wasn't alone). Before that voice, he said, he'd never felt so alone.

And then there is also the luck of the lesson. In the middle of praying for mercy on the icy hill, a cold clarity came into focus: nothing matters but this love. The house we were trying to buy, the car that will be ruined, the bills and the jobs, the slights and strivings and letdowns. None of it matters. All that matters is him and that he is okay and this baby inside me that we made. Let all the rest fall through the ice and freeze.

When we get home, he can't get warm. He takes a hot shower. I put more wood on the fire and fill a basin with near-scalding water for his feet. His hands and feet won't stop tingling. I call our neighbors Tim and Philip, who strung up white lanterns in the trees for our wedding, and they drop off soup for dinner. I tell L about the clarity I felt in the car and he says he felt it, too. *How do we hold on to that?* I ask. I'm always trying not to lose what I have.

We have tried not to lose it. We remind each other of it sometimes in the middle of job stress, in the middle of the pandemic. Usually it sounds like only words now, ideas without force, but every once in a while I can feel it again.

How much can you learn on the edge of losing everything? I don't want to find out what learning feels like on the other side of almost. But I know I will. As Oscar Wilde wrote in a letter, *hearts are made to be broken*. Life brings us all to our knees.

ONE NIGHT ON THE PHONE WITH SCOTT, I SAID, *WHAT happened to you*, as a reference to everything over the past six years—the crime, the arrest, the hearings, and the sentence. He said, *I don't think it's so much what happened to me but what I did*. And I said, *Well, maybe it's both—what happened and what you did*. Which is really what all of us could say about our lives.

For a while I was transfixed by Elizabeth Bishop's poem "Conversation," which is uncharacteristically abstract but still precise:

> *The tumult in the heart*
> *keeps asking questions.*
> *And then it stops and undertakes to answer*
> *in the same tone of voice.*
> *No one could tell the difference.*
>
> *Uninnocent, these conversations start,*
> *and then engage the senses,*

only half-meaning to.
And then there is no choice,
and then there is no sense;

until a name
and all its connotation are the same.

The word *uninnocent* is where Scott will always live. But it's where I feel at home, too. It's a big house, with many rooms and places to sleep, windows to let in the light. It is not a prison. There are no shackles. Here, mercy makes a door you can walk out of.

AS THE CAR WAS SKIDDING, L WAS AFRAID OF HITTING a tree. Instead, he ended up trapped under the ice. And when I started thinking about labor, I was scared of all the wrong things. At first, the giant needle, so I decided against an epidural. Then, *the ring of fire*, that moment right at the end, that final push. But these were not the hard parts. My pelvis didn't snap. What was hard was endurance, duration, *time*. We never know what to be afraid of.

When the contractions started, I tried to sleep through them. My first real contraction made me cry right away, from pain but also fear. *This can't be right*, I thought, *not so soon. Something must be wrong.* That was my first sleepless night. In the morning, we timed them. Ten minutes apart, then over the course of the day, seven, then five. We drove to the hospital with anticipation. But at the hospital, when the midwives checked my cervix, I was only half a centimeter dilated. They connected me to a monitor, and they could see the contractions were strong and regular. But they were *unproductive*, they said, and sent me home. I begged them to let me stay. They said I could walk around the hospital and try to move things along, but after two hours of walking around the empty hallways of the hospital at night, I'd dilated only a quarter of a centimeter more. They gave me an Ambien and sent me home.

At home, I labored in our bathroom and in the living room. All the pain was in my back. The Ambien didn't help me sleep and it didn't dull the pain. It only made me ramble in the bathtub incoherently about pies on the windowsill. Nights are endless without sleep. Darkness stopped the clock.

That night, our dog ate a whole chocolate cake, which L didn't tell me. We spent that night piled together on the living room floor, L afraid for us both. I couldn't eat; the pain made me throw up everything I tried.

At some point in the middle of the third night, I fell to my knees and prayed. I felt like I was stuck in a nightmare. I couldn't see the end. I'd lost track of who was on the other side. I remembered what my doula, Katie, who was splitting the nights with L, had told me when I first met her: every woman thinks, in the middle of a childbirth without medication, that she's going to die. She was right.

Early in the morning on the fourth day, I felt a leak. I was lying in bed, sleepless, with Katie asleep behind me. I stirred and when she woke up she said, *I just had a dream that everything is going to be okay.* I said, *I think my water broke.* I have never been so grateful for something breaking.

L and I made the forty-five-minute drive to the hospital again, this time in silence. My whole body was tender. Everything hurt. I winced every time we turned or drove over a pothole. I walked slowly from the car to the elevator and down the hall. Up in an examination room, the nurse tested me with a dye that turns blue if the amniotic sack is ruptured. I wanted to kiss that stain of blue dye.

But I was still only one centimeter dilated, so they gave me Pitocin and I asked for an epidural, which I was no longer afraid of. L tried to make sure I was thinking straight. I told him I had never been so sure of anything in my life. Right before the needle, I had half a Popsicle, and afterward I slept for seven hours while my cervix dilated from one to eight centimeters. When I woke up, they told me it was time to push, so I did. I pushed in rhythm with the contractions, which I could still feel but were no longer unbearable. The lights were down, everyone was concentrating and saying things like, *Keep going, almost there.* L's face hovered over me like a moon. They held a mirror between my legs so I could see the head, a new moon.

Suddenly—though it wasn't—someone said urgently, *Grab your baby*, and I didn't think, *How?* Or *In what way should I grab him?* Because at the sill of life and death there is no thought, only urge. I reached down and slung the baby onto my chest, as if he were a fish, bruised and wet. A piece of the amniotic sack lay intact on his cone-shaped head. They call this a *caul*, which comes from the Latin *Caput galeatum*, meaning *helmeted head*, a rare sign of good luck.

THERE YOU WERE, GOOD LUCK, BLUE FISH, SO SMALL and yet somehow much bigger than anything I'd held before.

What came to me was the somewhat grave and sober word *respect*. Also, the vast and joyful word *miracle*. I felt as if I'd been dropped down into the center of a mystery I didn't know I hadn't understood until I understood it.

I knew, then, that I would do it all again, all four days, a thousand times, to hold you in my arms. Because I couldn't love you until I held you, and to hold you I had to feel that edge and pray for mercy. I had to break open.

In the morning, I whisper two names down into your tiny face. When I say *Augustus*, you open your eyes. We call you Augie.

THE NOTION OF GOODNESS COMES INTO QUESTION quickly. *Is he a good baby?* people asked me, with a big smile. I knew it was harmless, but in the grips of wavering postpartum rage I wanted to shout, *WHAT DO YOU MEAN?* As a little girl, I worried whether I was good enough. Had I been good enough to earn the love that would keep me safe, keep things peaceful? A version of this worry has never left me.

Some portion of violence would be eradicated by people knowing their worth. Even Dylann Roof, who postures confidence by representing himself at his own trial and arguing his sanity, even he shakes with fear of unworthiness—a central ingredient in his racism. An underlying component of all racism. Distrust in our own worth is an early heartbreak that goes on and on, spreading heartbreak around like a virus.

If I could give my son anything, it would be this: certainty of worth. Certainty of worth without contingency or question. I want him to know that he doesn't need to earn love and mercy, because his life is not a debt or a hole that needs filling. Service and good work can be the fruit of this knowing. And when he needs it, when he joins the ranks of the undeserving, the uninnocent, which life turns us all into eventually—it's a matter of degrees that divides us, and maybe luck or something like it—I want him to remember that the mercy he asks for is his for the taking. The taking and the giving. Especially the giving.

From the Tibetan Book of the Dead: *O nobly born, O you of glorious origins, remember your radiant true nature.*

WHEN I READ CREIGH DEEDS'S STATEMENT—*I AM ALIVE so must live. Some wounds won't heal*—it felt like only a beginning. So the question *How do we go on?* remained. It's the force behind the sentences I started writing here.

I found one answer, or part of one, in the dark hospital

room on the night my son arrived and the world changed. The question is answered and the world changes every time a new life cracks through the clamor, shocked by light. He needed touch and warmth and food and love. Someone to hold him, something to hold. The urgency of this need doesn't dissipate with time.

But in our broken world, needs are thwarted. Love is the riskiest of all, a wanting and having that inevitably risks losing.

And when you lose someone you love or the life that you imagined, when you witness or feel violence or the violence of injustice, you might feel betrayed, bereaved of hope or faith. Your heart may skip or slacken.

This is heartbreak.

It may help to call it by its name.

And to remember that this feeling also ratifies the heart, your life—that is, the feeling is not separate from life, or outside time; it is what living feels like. Every day ends with the dying of the light. *The force behind the movement of time is a mourning that will not be comforted*, writes Marilynne Robinson in *Housekeeping*. Heartbreak is not a deviation from the script. It's a chapter in love's ongoingness through time.

CAVEAT: YOU WERE GIVEN LIFE AND LIFE GOES ON, but you don't have to. Ongoingness is a neutral force, but it's infused with meaning when you choose it. You have to choose it.

ON CHRISTMAS EVE, SCOTT EMAILS ME ABOUT A PRIS-
oner who tried to kill himself by lighting himself on fire.
He wasn't one of Scott's friends, but he knew him, had
seen him around. The living room at my parents' house is
full of family when I read the email to myself. Augie is shouting *pasta* because it's time for lunch. The sun is streaming
through the windows. Can you hold it all at once? The
man on fire and the bars on the windows and the sun in
winter and the baby who has more than he needs screaming *More*. Can you choose it, turning no feeling or fact
away? Can you hold on to the enterprise under way in your
chest?

That night, as I set out presents underneath the tree for
Augie to find in the morning—a wooden car, some tiny animals, and new crayons—I'm suddenly thinking of Ryan.
This is something that still happens. I think of his hands,
now that I know what little boys' hands are like, dirty and
sweet. I think of his hands fighting back. What would Ryan
want for Christmas? What would he tell us if he could? No
answer. Only the not-quite silence of the room lit by a tree
strung with lights like stars, and outside, the not-quite silence of snow and animals sleeping, some waking up to hunt.

From "Music Is in the Piano Only When It Is Played," a
poem by Jack Gilbert:

God does not live among the church bells,
but is briefly resident there. We are occasional
like that. A lifetime of easy happiness mixed
with pain and loss, trying always to name and hold
on to the enterprise under way in our chest.

A few days later, Augie and I wake up to a cacophony in the sky. I pick him up and we run to the windows. Hundreds of seagulls, plunging and diving and coasting and squawking, in from the lake to find food. They swoop past us, their bellies and underwings lit by a half-risen sun weakened by winter, dreamlike against slate clouds, everything gold and gray. Delight breaks over us and Augie begins to laugh. Church bells, I think. Out past the seagulls the horizon goes on and on. Nothing is spared. I choose it anyway.

SOURCES AND RESOURCES

2011 Louisiana Laws, Revised Statutes, Title 14, Criminal Law, RS 14:30, *First degree murder* (LA Rev Stat § 14:30).

Aitken, Will. "Anne Carson, The Art of Poetry No. 88." *The Paris Review* 171 (Fall 2004).

Allen, James, et al. *Without Sanctuary: Lynching Photography in America*. Santa Fe, NM: Twin Palms, 2000.

Augustine of Hippo. *The Confessions of St. Augustine: Books I–IX (Selections)*. New York: Prentice-Hall, 1931. Later, the Augustinian order adopted as its emblem a heart on fire, shot through by an arrow.

Berryman, John. "To Bhain Campbell." *The Art of Losing: Poems of Grief and Healing*. Edited by Kevin Young. New York: Bloomsbury USA, 2013.

Bishop, Elizabeth. "Conversation." *The Complete Poems, 1927–1979*. New York: Farrar, Straus and Giroux, 1983.

Blake, Michelle. "One Day." *Into the Wide and Startling World*. Georgetown: Finishing Line Press, 2012.

Boyer, Anne. *The Undying: Pain, Vulnerability, Mortality, Medicine, Art, Time, Dreams, Data, Exhaustion, Cancer, and Care*. New York: Farrar, Straus and Giroux, 2019.

Chabon, Michael. *The Amazing Adventures of Kavalier & Clay*. New York: Random House, 2000.

Children's Defense Fund. *Protect Children Not Guns, 2019*, https://www.childrensdefense.org/policy/resources/protect-children-not-guns.

Didion, Joan. *Slouching Towards Bethlehem*. New York: Farrar, Straus and Giroux, 1968. The title of the collection and the notion of the center not holding both come from William Butler Yeats's poem "The Second Coming."

Dreher, Rod. "'Wayne, I Accept Your Curse. I'm the Dad.'" *The American Conservative*, August 27, 2013.

Fisher, Helen E., et al. "Reward, Addiction, and Emotion Regulation Systems Associated with Rejection in Love." *Journal of Neurophysiology* 104, no. 1 (2010): 51–60; doi:10.1152/jn.00784.2009.

Ghansah, Rachel Kaadzi. "A Most American Terrorist: The Making of Dylann Roof." *GQ*, August 21, 2017.

Gilbert, Jack. "Music Is in the Piano Only When It Is Played." *Refusing Heaven*. New York: Alfred A. Knopf, 2007.

Gilligan, James. *Violence: Reflections on a National Epidemic*. New York: Vintage Books, 1997.

Groff, Lauren. "The Wind." *The New Yorker*, February 1, 2021.

Hindson, Edward, and Ed Dobson. "Why Preachers' Kids Go Bad." *SOR Faculty Publications and Presentations* 140 (1983): 12–13.

Howe, Fanny. "Buddhists Like School and I Don't." *Poetry Magazine*, March 2009.

Jauhar, Sandeep. *Heart: A History*. New York: Farrar, Straus and Giroux, 2018.

Johnson, Corey G. "Bryan Stevenson on Charleston and Our Real Problem with Race." *The Marshall Project*, June 24, 2015.

Jung, C. G. *Collected Works of C. G. Jung, Volume 9, Part 2: Aion: Researches into the Phenomenology of the Self*. Edited and translated by Gerhard Adler and R. F. C. Hull. Princeton, NJ: Princeton University Press, 1959. "The psychological rule says that when an inner situation is not made conscious, it happens outside as fate. That is to say, when the individual remains undivided and does not become conscious of his inner opposite, the world must perforce act out the conflict."

Karma-gliṅ-pa. *The Tibetan Book of the Dead: The Great Liberation through Hearing in the Bardo*. Translated by Francesca Fremantle and Chögyam Trungpa. Boulder, CO: Shambhala, 1992.

Kornfield, Jack. *After the Ecstasy, the Laundry: How the Heart Grows Wise on the Spiritual Path*. New York: Bantam Dell, 2001.

Kross, Ethan, et al. "Social Rejection Shares Somatosensory Representations with Physical Pain." *Proceedings of the National Academy of Sciences of the United States of America* 108, no. 15 (2011): 6270–75; doi:10.1073/pnas.1102693108.

Machado, Carmen Maria. *In the Dream House*. Minneapolis: Graywolf Press, 2019.

Manguso, Sarah. *300 Arguments*. Minneapolis: Graywolf Press, 2017.

Marinković, Slobodan, et al. "Heart in Anatomy History, Radiology, Anthropology and Art." *Folia Morphologica* 73, no. 2 (2014): 103–12, https://www.researchgate.net/publication/262564742_Heart_in_anatomy _history_radiology_anthropology_and_art#pf2.

Martin, Rachel. "Caring for a Schizophrenic Son, Worrying About the Future." NPR, November 24, 2013, https://www.npr.org/transcripts /246904487.

Myss, Caroline. "Carolyn Myss: The Courage to Confront Evil." *Insights at the Edge with Tami Simon*, podcast, October 15, 2019.

Nelson, Maggie. *The Red Parts: Autobiography of a Trial*. Minneapolis: Graywolf Press, 2007.

O'Neill, Eugene. *The Iceman Cometh*. New Haven, CT: Yale University Press, 2006, 1939.

Pant, Sadip, et al. "Clustering of Takotsubo Cardiomyopathy Cases in United States in 2011." *Journal of the American College of Cardiology* 63, no. 12 (2014): A828; doi:10.1016/S0735-1097(14)60828-7.

Peelen, Mary. "Prognosis." *Quantum Heresies*. Glenview, IL: Glass Lyre Press, 2019.

Rhodes, Larry A. "The Heart and Its Electrical System." *Heart Matters*, 2008.

Robinson, Marilynne. *Gilead*. New York: Farrar, Straus and Giroux, 2014.

———. *Housekeeping*. New York: Picador, 2004.

Roper v. Simmons, 543 U.S. 551 (2005).

Rovner, Josh. *Juvenile Life Without Parole: An Overview*. Washington, DC: The Sentencing Project, 2021.

Sack, Kevin, and Alan Blinder. "Jurors Hear Dylann Roof Explain Shooting in Video: 'I Had to Do It.'" *New York Times*, December 9, 2016.

Schjeldahl, Peter. "All Souls." *The New Yorker*, October 27, 2007.

Segura, Liliana. "Henry Montgomery Paved the Way for Other Juvenile Lifers to Go Free. Now 72, He May Never Get the Same Chance." *The Intercept*, June 2, 2019.

Sendrow, Michael. "Second Hand Victims." *Medium*, March 30, 2018, https://medium.com/@michaelsendrow/secondhand-victims-720406fe3795.

Senghor, Shaka. *Writing My Wrongs: Life, Death, and Redemption in an American Prison*. New York: Convergent Books, 2017.

Solnit, Rebecca. *A Paradise Built in Hell: The Extraordinary Communities That Arise in Disaster*. New York: Penguin Books, 2009.

Stanford v. Kentucky, 492 U.S. 361 (1989).

Stevenson, Bryan. *Just Mercy*. New York: Spiegel & Grau, 2014.

Sullivan, Erin. "Shakespeare and the History of Heartbreak." *The Art of Medicine* 382, no. 9896 (2013): 933–34; doi:10.1016/S0140-6736(13)61923-6.

Szymborska, Wisława. "Could Have." *View with a Grain of Sand*. Translated by Stanislaw Baranczak and Clare Cavanagh. New York: Harcourt, Brace, 1996.

The ETCSL Project. "The Electronic Text Corpus of Sumerian Literature." Last updated 2006, https://etcsl.orinst.ox.ac.uk.

The Innocence Project. "Why Do Innocent People Plead Guilty?," http://www.guiltypleaproblem.org.

Thompson, Dennis. "Grief May Trigger Heart Rhythm Trouble." *HealthDay News*, April 6, 2016.

W., Bill. *Alcoholics Anonymous: The Story of How Many Thousands of Men and Women Have Recovered from Alcoholism*. New York: Alcoholics Anonymous World Services, 1976.

World Health Organization. *International Classification of Diseases for Mortality and Morbidity Statistics*, 11th revision. 2018.

ACKNOWLEDGMENTS

Writing requires time and space. Thank you to Heather Evans and Annie Barkan for giving me time by taking care of Augie. Thank you for teaching me what care really means. As for space, most of this writing took place at the Burlington Fletcher Free Library and Zabby & Elf's. I'm grateful to the people who kept the lights and heat on in both these places.

To my agent, Gail Hochman, thank you for shepherding me along with such warmth and wisdom. You believed in a book here before anyone else did. Thank you to Laird Gallagher, for taking a chance. Thank you to my editor, Jackson Howard, for your discernment, honesty, faith, and attention. You're cooler than I'll ever be and I love your brain. And thank you to the whole team at FSG and FSG Originals—including Brianna Panzica, Andrea Monagle, Janet Renard, Kathleen Cook, Janet Evans-Scanlon, Alexis Nowicki, and Adrienne Davis—what an honor it has been to land here with you.

Thank you to my teachers and friends who told me I could and should write throughout the years of not writing and beginning: Robert Hosmer, Sarah London, Annie Chagnot, Viola Canales, Jeanne Merino, Julian Simcock, S. Abbas Raza, Paul Sonne, Courtney Weaver, Pamela Post-Ferrante, Dorian Fox, Caroline Grey. What you said mattered; I carried it with me. And thank you to my readers and editors: Caroline, Courtney, Liza Cochran, Tarik Bolat, and especially Kathryn McCann Newhall and Kate Makhzoumi.

Thank you to Stanford Law School and the professors there who taught me about justice, especially Joan Petersilia, Robert Weisberg, Debbie Mukamal, Jeff Strnad, Jonathan Zittrain, and Ralph Richard Banks. Thank you to the women of the Stanford Community Law Clinic, who showed me what justice looks like in the living, breathing world: Juliet Brodie, Danielle Jones, Lisa Douglass, Nisha Vyas, and Lupe Buenrostro.

For their tirelessness and faith in a more just world, I'm grateful to have had the chance to learn from Marian Wright Edelman and the whole Children's Defense Fund, especially Chris Glaros and Rev. Dr. Janet Wolf; David Fathi and the attorneys at the National Prison Project; the teachers and organizers at Mount Tamalpais College; and most especially Bryan Stevenson, whom I am certain history will understand to be one of our brightest lights.

I'm also grateful to Dan Berman; Michael Sendrow; Dr. Gorscak and the Center for Complicated Grief; Inge Hansen, for seeing me through; Nicky Lewenson, for saving me twice; Lorni, for sharing her pain and strength; and BN, for everything.

To my family who do and don't appear in these pages, this is for and because of you. Thank you to my mother-in-law, Susan Brophy, for your loving guidance, pesto, and camaraderie; to my brother, Sam McFarland, for telling me that I'm strong and for showing me what strength looks like; to my parents, Michelle Blake and Dennis McFarland, thank you for filling our home with books, stories, and poems, for teaching me how to take pains, for your healing, sacrifice, confidence, and blessing. I love you.

To Luke, my heart, my rock, first believer, and best reader, I hope it goes on and on. Augie, you are ours and your own, my untamed teacher; thank you for choosing us.

Alexander Chee says to write for your dead. I wrote for Garnette, Tellis, Nezzy, and Alice. Now I'll write for Michael, too, who was a teacher beyond compare, whose brain was bested only by his heart. There are many other spirits who fill these pages—this is for you, too.

PERMISSIONS ACKNOWLEDGMENTS

Grateful acknowledgment is made for permission to reprint the following material:

Excerpt from "In prison" by Jean Valentine, from *Break the Glass*. Originally published in *The New Yorker* (May 27, 2007). Copyright © 2007, 2010 by Jean Valentine. Reprinted with the permission of The Permissions Company, LLC, on behalf of Copper Canyon Press, coppercanyonpress.org.

Excerpt from *Housekeeping* by Marilynne Robinson. Copyright © 1981 by Marilynne Robinson. Reprinted by permission of Farrar, Straus and Giroux.

Excerpt from *Housekeeping*, copyright © Marilynne Robinson and reproduced by permission of Faber & Faber Ltd.

Excerpt from "Jim Limber in Heaven Is a Nexus at Which Many Heavens of the Multiverse Converge" from *Sometimes I Never Suffered* by Shane McCrae. Copyright © 2010 by Shane McCrae. Reprinted by permission of Farrar, Straus and Giroux.

Excerpt from "Jim Limber in Heaven Is a Nexus at Which Many Heavens of the Multiverse Converge" from *Sometimes I Never Suffered* by Shane McCrae. Copyright © 2010 by Shane McCrae. Reprinted by permission of Little Brown Group Ltd, United Kingdom.

"To Bhain Campbell" from *Collected Poems: 1937–1971* by John Berryman. Copyright © 1989 by Kate Donahue Berryman. Reprinted by permission of Farrar, Straus and Giroux.

"Conversation" from *Poems* by Elizabeth Bishop. Copyright © 2011 by The Alice H. Methfessel Trust. Publisher's Note and compilation copyright © 2011 by Farrar, Straus and Giroux. Reprinted by permission of Farrar, Straus and Giroux.

"Conversation" from *Poems* by Elizabeth Bishop, published by Chatto & Windus. Copyright © 2011 Alice H. Methfessel Trust. Reprinted by permission of The Random House Group Limited.